SARA L. WESTON

The Narcissist Repellent

"In the aftermath of a covert narcissist's behavior, resentment festers, but redemption becomes the antidote. Through the shards of broken trust, recovery is a battle waged. Scarred yet resolute, we emerge, rewriting our story beyond the manipulative grasp of the covert narcissist, forging a path of self-discovery and resilience."

Contents

Foreword

J. Something good from the trail of destruction you left behind.

Preface

"In the absence of a narcissistic repellent, this book emerges as a compass, a guide for those navigating the labyrinth of relationships tainted by Narcissistic Personality Styles. Recognizing the challenges faced in love, work, or family dynamics, these pages aim to shed light on the intricate dance with narcissism. Through insights and understanding, this preface invites you to embark on a journey of self-discovery and healing. May the following chapters offer clarity, resilience, and a pathway toward reclaiming your own narrative in the presence of narcissistic influences."

1

Chapter 1

Introduction to Narcissistic Personality Styles

1.1 Understanding Narcissistic Personality Disorder

Narcissistic Personality Disorder (NPD) is a complex and often misunderstood mental health condition characterized by an inflated sense of self-importance, a constant need for admiration, and a lack of empathy for others. Individuals with NPD exhibit a range of traits and behaviors that can be categorized into two main styles: Covert Narcissism and Overt Narcissism. Understanding these styles and the variations in severity and presentations is crucial in recognizing and dealing with narcissistic individuals in various aspects of life.

1.1.1 Covert Narcissism: Recognizing the Hidden Traits

Covert Narcissism refers to a more subtle and less obvious form of narcissism. Individuals with covert narcissism often present themselves as shy, introverted, and even self-deprecating, making it challenging to identify their narcissistic tendencies. However, beneath this facade lies a deep-seated need for validation and a sense of superiority. Some common traits associated with covert narcissism include:

1. **Victim Mentality**: Covert narcissists often portray themselves as victims, constantly seeking sympathy and attention from others. They may manipulate situations to gain sympathy and use it as a means to control and manipulate others.
2. **Passive-Aggressive Behavior**: Covert narcissists tend to express their aggression indirectly, using subtle tactics such as sarcasm, backhanded compliments, and silent treatment. They may also engage in covert manipulation to maintain control over others.
3. **Excessive Sensitivity**: Covert narcissists are highly sensitive to criticism and rejection, often reacting with intense emotional outbursts or withdrawing from social interactions altogether. They may also use their sensitivity as a means to manipulate others and gain sympathy.
4. **Grandiosity in Private**: While covert narcissists may appear humble and self-effacing in public, they harbor grandiose fantasies and a sense of entitlement in private. They believe they are special and deserving of admiration, but they keep this hidden to avoid scrutiny.

1.1.2 Overt Narcissism: Identifying the Obvious Traits

Overt Narcissism, on the other hand, is characterized by more overt and grandiose behaviors. Individuals with overt narcissism have an inflated sense of self-importance and openly seek admiration and attention from others. Some common traits associated with overt narcissism include:

1. **Grandiose Self-Image**: Overt narcissists have an exaggerated sense of self-importance and believe they are superior to others. They constantly seek validation and admiration to reinforce their self-worth.
2. **Lack of Empathy**: Overt narcissists have a limited capacity for empathy and struggle to understand or relate to the emotions and experiences of others. They often disregard the feelings and needs of those around them.

3. **Exploitative Behavior**: Overt narcissists have a tendency to exploit others for their own gain. They may manipulate, deceive, or use others to achieve their goals without any regard for the well-being of those they exploit.

4. **Attention-Seeking**: Overt narcissists crave constant attention and admiration. They often engage in attention-seeking behaviors such as boasting, exaggerating their achievements, and seeking validation from others.

1.1.3 Variations in Severity and Presentations of Narcissistic Personality Styles

Narcissistic Personality Styles can vary in severity and presentations, making it important to understand the different manifestations of narcissism. Some individuals may exhibit more subtle narcissistic traits, while others may display more extreme and destructive behaviors. It is crucial to recognize that narcissism exists on a spectrum, and not all individuals with narcissistic traits will meet the criteria for Narcissistic Personality Disorder.

The severity of narcissistic traits can range from mild to severe, with some individuals displaying occasional narcissistic behaviors, while others exhibit a pervasive pattern of narcissistic traits in all areas of their life. Additionally, the presentation of narcissism can differ based on cultural, societal, and individual factors. Some individuals may display more overt narcissistic traits, while others may exhibit covert narcissistic tendencies.

Understanding the variations in severity and presentations of narcissistic personality styles can help individuals identify and navigate relationships with narcissistic individuals more effectively. It is important to remember that while narcissistic traits can be challenging to deal with, it is possible to establish healthy boundaries and protect oneself from the negative impact of these relationships.

In the following chapters, we will explore the impact of narcissism in various aspects of life, including romantic relationships, family dynamics, friendships, and the workplace. We will also delve into strategies for self-preservation, healing, and recovery, as well as prevention and self-protection to avoid getting involved in relationships with narcissists. By gaining a deeper understanding of narcissistic personality styles, we can empower ourselves to navigate these challenging dynamics and foster healthier relationships.

1.2 Covert Narcissism

Covert narcissism is a lesser-known form of narcissistic personality style that often goes unnoticed due to its subtle and hidden traits. While overt narcissists display their grandiosity and seek constant attention, covert narcissists operate in a more covert and manipulative manner. They may appear shy, introverted, or even selfless on the surface, but underneath lies a deep sense of entitlement and a need for admiration.

1.2.1 Understanding Covert Narcissism

Covert narcissists possess many of the same traits as their overt counterparts but express them in a more understated and covert manner. They are masters of manipulation, using subtle tactics to control and exploit others for their own gain. Unlike overt narcissists who seek the spotlight, covert narcissists prefer to operate behind the scenes, exerting their influence in more subtle ways.

One of the key characteristics of covert narcissism is a strong sense of entitlement. They believe they deserve special treatment and attention, but instead of demanding it openly, they manipulate others into meeting their needs. Covert narcissists often play the victim, using guilt and pity to gain sympathy and control over others. They may appear selfless and caring, but their actions are driven by a desire for personal gain and admiration.

1.2.2 Recognizing Covert Narcissistic Traits

Identifying covert narcissistic traits can be challenging, as they often present themselves as kind, empathetic, and selfless individuals. However, there are subtle signs that can help you recognize covert narcissism:

1. **Excessive need for validation**: Covert narcissists crave constant reassurance and validation from others. They may fish for compliments or subtly manipulate situations to receive praise and admiration.
2. **Lack of empathy**: While covert narcissists may appear empathetic on the surface, their empathy is often superficial. They struggle to truly understand and connect with the emotions of others, as their primary focus is on their own needs and desires.
3. **Manipulative behavior**: Covert narcissists are skilled manipulators. They use subtle tactics such as guilt-tripping, gaslighting, and emotional manipulation to control and exploit others.
4. **Fragile self-esteem**: Despite their outward appearance of confidence, covert narcissists have fragile self-esteem. They are highly sensitive to criticism and rejection, and may react with anger or defensiveness when their ego is threatened.
5. **Lack of accountability**: Covert narcissists rarely take responsibility for their actions. They deflect blame onto others and refuse to acknowledge their mistakes or shortcomings.

1.2.3 Variations in Severity and Presentations

Just like overt narcissism, covert narcissism exists on a spectrum, with varying degrees of severity and presentations. Some individuals may exhibit only a few covert narcissistic traits, while others may display a full-blown covert narcissistic personality disorder.

The severity of covert narcissism can range from mild to severe, with the more severe cases often causing significant distress and harm to those around them. It is important to note that covert narcissism can coexist with other mental health conditions, such as anxiety or depression, which can further complicate the presentation and treatment.

In terms of presentations, covert narcissists can vary in their behavior and tactics. Some may use passive-aggressive tactics, such as silent treatment or withholding affection, to manipulate and control others. Others may present themselves as selfless and caring individuals, using their apparent kindness as a means to gain admiration and control.

1.2.4 Covert Narcissism in Males, Females, and the GLBTQI Community

Covert narcissism can be found in individuals of all genders and sexual orientations. However, societal expectations and stereotypes can influence the way covert narcissism manifests in different groups.

In males, covert narcissism may be more prevalent due to societal pressures to appear strong and self-sufficient. Male covert narcissists may mask their insecurities and need for admiration by projecting an image of stoicism and selflessness. They may use their perceived vulnerability to manipulate and control others, often in intimate relationships.

Similarly, females with covert narcissism may present themselves as nurturing and selfless individuals, conforming to societal expectations of femininity. They may use their apparent vulnerability and need for support to gain sympathy and control over others.

In the GLBTQI community, covert narcissism can present unique challenges. The pressure to conform to societal norms and expectations can exacerbate the covert narcissistic traits in individuals. It is important to recognize and address covert narcissism within the GLBTQI community to foster healthy and supportive relationships.

Conclusion

Understanding covert narcissism is crucial for recognizing and protecting oneself from the manipulative tactics of individuals with this personality style. By being aware of the subtle signs and variations in presentations, we can empower ourselves to navigate relationships with covert narcissists more effectively. In the following chapters, we will explore how covert narcissism manifests in romantic relationships, friendships, and the workplace, as well as strategies for self-preservation and healing.

1.3 Overt Narcissism

Overt narcissism refers to the more obvious and grandiose traits associated with narcissistic personality styles. Individuals with overt narcissism tend to display their self-centeredness and need for admiration in a more overt and exaggerated manner. They often seek attention and validation from others, and their behavior can be easily recognized as narcissistic.

1.3.1 Grandiosity and Exaggerated Self-Importance

One of the key traits of overt narcissism is a grandiose sense of self-importance. Individuals with overt narcissism often have an inflated view of their own abilities, achievements, and importance. They believe they are superior to others and expect special treatment and recognition. They may constantly seek praise and admiration, and they may exaggerate their accomplishments or talents to gain attention and validation.

1.3.2 Need for Constant Attention and Admiration

Individuals with overt narcissism have an insatiable need for attention and admiration. They constantly seek validation and approval from others and may go to great lengths to ensure they are the center of attention. They may engage in attention-seeking behaviors such as boasting, bragging, or exaggerating their achievements. They may also demand constant praise and admiration from others, and become upset or angry if they feel ignored or overlooked.

1.3.3 Lack of Empathy and Exploitative Behavior

Overt narcissists often lack empathy and have little regard for the feelings or needs of others. They may exploit and manipulate others to meet their own needs and desires. They may use charm and charisma to manipulate and control others, and may engage in manipulative tactics such as gaslighting or emotional manipulation. They may also take advantage of others' vulnerabilities for personal gain, without any remorse or guilt.

1.3.4 Sense of Entitlement and Boundary Violations

Individuals with overt narcissism often have a strong sense of entitlement and believe they deserve special treatment and privileges. They may disregard the boundaries and needs of others, and may expect others to cater to their every whim. They may become angry or resentful if their demands are not met, and may engage in entitled behaviors such as demanding special favors, expecting others to always put their needs first, or disregarding the feelings and boundaries of others.

1.3.5 Aggression and Narcissistic Rage

Overt narcissists may display aggression and anger when their grandiose self-image is threatened or when they feel criticized or rejected. They may react with narcissistic rage, which can manifest as explosive outbursts, verbal attacks, or even physical violence. This aggression is often a defense mechanism to protect their fragile self-esteem and maintain their sense of superiority.

1.3.6 Variations in Severity and Presentations

It is important to note that narcissistic personality styles can vary in severity and presentations. Some individuals may exhibit overt narcissistic traits more prominently, while others may display a combination of overt and covert traits. The severity of narcissistic traits can also vary, with some individuals exhibiting more extreme and destructive behaviors than others.

1.3.7 Gender and Narcissism

Narcissistic personality styles can be observed in both males and females. While there may be some differences in the way narcissism is expressed based on societal expectations and gender roles, the core traits and behaviors associated with narcissism remain the same. It is important to recognize that narcissism is not limited to a specific gender and can be found in individuals of all genders.

1.3.8 Narcissism in the GLBTQI Community

Narcissistic personality styles can also be observed within the GLBTQI community. The unique challenges and perspectives within this community can influence the manifestation of narcissistic traits. It is important to understand and address narcissism within the GLBTQI community to provide appropriate support and resources for individuals who may be affected by narcissistic abuse.

In the next chapter, we will explore the red flags to look out for when dating and how to identify potential partners with narcissistic personality styles. We will also discuss strategies for understanding and surviving relationships with narcissists, as well as looking after yourself and healing after the end of a relationship with a narcissist.

1.4 Variations in Severity and Presentations of Narcissistic Personality Styles

Narcissistic personality styles can manifest in various ways, with different levels of severity and presentations. Understanding these variations is crucial in recognizing and dealing with individuals who exhibit narcissistic traits. Whether it is the overt or covert style, both can have a significant impact on relationships and the well-being of those involved.

1.4.1 The Spectrum of Narcissistic Personality Styles

Narcissistic personality styles exist on a spectrum, ranging from mild to severe. At one end of the spectrum, individuals may display subtle narcissistic traits, while at the other end, the traits may be more pronounced and disruptive. It is important to note that not all individuals with narcissistic traits will meet the criteria for Narcissistic Personality Disorder (NPD), but their behavior can still have a significant impact on those around them.

1.4.2 Overt Narcissism: Obvious Traits and Behaviors

Overt narcissism is characterized by grandiosity, a need for admiration, and a lack of empathy. Individuals with overt narcissistic traits often seek attention and validation, and they may display their superiority and entitlement openly. They may engage in self-promotion, exaggerate their achievements, and belittle others to maintain their sense of superiority. Their behavior can be easily recognizable, as they often dominate conversations, seek constant praise, and have a sense of entitlement.

1.4.3 Covert Narcissism: Hidden Traits and Behaviors

Covert narcissism, also known as vulnerable narcissism, is characterized by a more subtle presentation of narcissistic traits. Individuals with covert narcissistic traits may appear shy, introverted, or even self-deprecating.

However, beneath this facade, they harbor a deep sense of entitlement, a need for admiration, and a lack of empathy. They may manipulate others through guilt, play the victim, and engage in passive-aggressive behaviors to maintain control and attention.

1.4.4 Gender and Narcissistic Personality Styles

Narcissistic personality styles can be observed in both males and females, although the presentation may differ due to societal expectations and stereotypes. In males, narcissistic traits may be more overtly displayed, aligning with traditional notions of dominance and power. In females, narcissistic traits may be expressed covertly, as societal expectations often discourage women from openly seeking attention and power. It is important to recognize that narcissism is not limited to a specific gender and can manifest in various ways.

1.4.5 Narcissism in the GLBTQI Community

Narcissistic personality styles can also be observed within the GLBTQI community. The unique challenges faced by individuals in this community can contribute to the development of narcissistic traits. These challenges may include societal discrimination, internalized homophobia, and the pressure to conform to certain stereotypes. Understanding the intersectionality of narcissism and the GLBTQI community is crucial in providing support and addressing the specific needs of individuals within this community.

1.4.6 Variations in Severity and Impact on Relationships

The severity of narcissistic personality styles can vary greatly, and this has a direct impact on relationships. Individuals with mild narcissistic traits may exhibit occasional self-centered behaviors, while those with severe narcissistic traits may engage in manipulative and abusive behaviors. It is important to recognize the red flags and early warning signs of narcissistic behavior in order to protect oneself from potential harm.

1.4.7 Red Flags in Romantic Relationships

When entering into a romantic relationship, it is essential to be aware of the red flags that may indicate the presence of narcissistic traits. These red flags can include excessive self-focus, a lack of empathy, a need for constant admiration, and a tendency to manipulate and control. It is important to trust your instincts and not dismiss these warning signs, as they can be indicative of a potentially toxic and abusive relationship.

1.4.8 Managing Narcissistic Relatives, Bosses, and Friends

Narcissistic personality styles can extend beyond romantic relationships and impact other areas of life, such as relationships with relatives, bosses, and friends. Strategies for managing these relationships include setting boundaries, practicing assertiveness, and seeking support from trusted individuals. It is important to prioritize self-care and protect one's emotional well-being when dealing with individuals who exhibit narcissistic traits.

In conclusion, narcissistic personality styles can vary in severity and presentation, with both overt and covert styles having a significant impact on relationships and well-being. Recognizing the red flags in romantic relationships, managing relationships with narcissistic relatives, bosses, and friends, and understanding the unique challenges faced by the GLBTQI community are essential in navigating and surviving interactions with individuals who exhibit narcissistic traits. By empowering oneself with knowledge and support, it is possible to protect one's emotional well-being and build healthier relationships.

2

Chapter 2

Narcissism in Relationships

2.1 Narcissism in Romantic Relationships

Romantic relationships are a common arena where narcissistic personality styles can manifest and cause significant distress for the individuals involved. It is crucial to understand the red flags and warning signs associated with narcissism to protect oneself from potential harm. This section will explore the dynamics of narcissism in romantic relationships, including the traits commonly exhibited by narcissists and strategies for identifying and avoiding these individuals.

Understanding Narcissistic Personality Styles in Romantic Relationships

Narcissistic personality styles can be categorized into two main types: covert and overt. Covert narcissists tend to be more subtle in their behaviors, often presenting themselves as victims or martyrs. They may manipulate their partners emotionally, using guilt and pity to gain control. On the other hand, overt narcissists display grandiose and attention-seeking behaviors, constantly seeking admiration and validation from their partners.

Both covert and overt narcissists share common traits that can be detrimental to romantic relationships. These traits include a lack of empathy, an excessive need for admiration, a sense of entitlement, and a tendency to exploit others for personal gain. Narcissists often struggle with intimacy and have difficulty forming genuine emotional connections with their partners. They may also exhibit controlling and manipulative behaviors, such as gaslighting, to maintain power and control in the relationship.

Red Flags to Look Out For

Recognizing the red flags associated with narcissistic behavior is essential in protecting oneself from entering into a harmful romantic relationship. While it is important to approach relationships with an open mind, being aware of these warning signs can help individuals make informed decisions about their partners. Some common red flags include:

1. Excessive self-centeredness: Narcissists often prioritize their own needs and desires above those of their partners. They may consistently disregard or dismiss their partner's feelings and opinions.
2. Lack of empathy: Narcissists struggle to understand and empathize with their partner's emotions. They may dismiss or belittle their partner's feelings, making them feel invalidated and unimportant.
3. Constant need for validation: Narcissists crave constant admiration and validation from their partners. They may seek attention and praise

from others, often at the expense of their partner's well-being.

4. Manipulative behavior: Narcissists are skilled manipulators and may use tactics such as gaslighting, guilt-tripping, or emotional blackmail to control their partners and maintain power in the relationship.

5. Lack of accountability: Narcissists often refuse to take responsibility for their actions and may deflect blame onto their partners or others. They may also exhibit a sense of entitlement, expecting special treatment without reciprocating.

6. Intense jealousy and possessiveness: Narcissists may display extreme jealousy and possessiveness, attempting to control their partner's actions and isolate them from friends and family.

7. Rapid idealization and devaluation: Narcissists tend to idealize their partners in the early stages of the relationship, showering them with attention and affection. However, this idealization is often short-lived, and they may quickly devalue their partner, criticizing and demeaning them.

Identifying Potential Partners

To avoid getting involved in romantic relationships with narcissists, it is crucial to develop a keen sense of self-awareness and establish healthy boundaries. Here are some strategies for identifying potential partners who may exhibit narcissistic traits:

1. Take your time: Rushing into a relationship can make it difficult to see the warning signs. Take the time to get to know your partner and observe their behavior in various situations.

2. Pay attention to their actions: Actions speak louder than words. Observe how your potential partner treats others, especially those in vulnerable positions, such as service staff or animals. Narcissists often display a lack of empathy and respect for others.

3. Trust your instincts: If something feels off or too good to be true, trust your gut instincts. Narcissists are skilled at manipulating and charming

others, but your intuition can often sense when something is not right.

4. Seek feedback from trusted friends and family: Sometimes, those close to us can see things that we may overlook. Share your concerns with trusted friends or family members and listen to their perspectives.

5. Look for consistency: Narcissists often exhibit inconsistent behavior, alternating between extreme charm and coldness. Pay attention to any patterns of inconsistency in your potential partner's actions and words.

Remember, it is not your fault if you find yourself in a relationship with a narcissist. Many individuals have fallen victim to their manipulative tactics. The most important thing is to prioritize your well-being and take steps to protect yourself.

In the next section, we will explore strategies for understanding and surviving relationships with narcissists, including how to look after yourself and heal after the relationship ends.

2.2 Dating and Narcissistic Personality Styles

Dating can be an exciting and exhilarating experience, but it can also be a minefield, especially when it comes to navigating relationships with individuals who exhibit narcissistic personality styles. Narcissists are individuals who have an inflated sense of self-importance, a constant need for admiration, and a lack of empathy for others. They can be charming and charismatic, making it difficult to recognize their true nature until it's too late. In this chapter, we will explore the red flags to look out for when dating, as well as strategies for identifying potential partners with narcissistic traits.

Recognizing the Red Flags

When entering the dating scene, it's important to be aware of the warning signs that may indicate a potential partner has narcissistic tendencies. While not all individuals who exhibit these traits are narcissists, these red flags can serve as a starting point for further exploration:

1. **Excessive self-focus**: Narcissists often dominate conversations, constantly steering the topic back to themselves. They may show little interest in getting to know you on a deeper level.
2. **Grandiose sense of self**: Pay attention to individuals who consistently boast about their achievements, talents, or possessions. They may exaggerate their accomplishments or belittle others to elevate themselves.
3. **Lack of empathy**: Narcissists struggle to understand or care about the feelings and needs of others. They may dismiss or invalidate your emotions, making you feel unheard or unimportant.
4. **Manipulative behavior**: Watch out for individuals who use manipulation tactics to control or exploit you. They may employ gaslighting, guilt-tripping, or other forms of emotional manipulation to maintain power and control in the relationship.
5. **Sense of entitlement**: Narcissists often believe they deserve special treatment and privileges. They may expect you to cater to their needs and desires without reciprocating.
6. **Superficial charm**: Narcissists can be incredibly charming and charismatic, especially during the early stages of a relationship. However, this charm may mask their true intentions and lack of genuine emotional connection.

Identifying Potential Partners with Narcissistic Traits

While it's not always possible to identify a narcissist with certainty during the early stages of dating, there are certain traits and behaviors that may indicate a higher likelihood. These traits can help you make more informed decisions about whether to pursue a relationship with someone:

1. **Excessive self-promotion**: Pay attention to individuals who consistently seek attention and validation from others. They may use social media as a platform to showcase their achievements and garner admiration.
2. **Lack of accountability**: Narcissists often struggle to take responsibility

for their actions and may deflect blame onto others. They may have a history of failed relationships or a pattern of blaming their ex-partners for the relationship's demise.

3. **Unrealistic expectations**: Be cautious of individuals who have unrealistic expectations of what a relationship should be. They may have an idealized view of love and expect their partner to fulfill all their needs and desires.

4. **Love-bombing**: Narcissists often employ a tactic called "love-bombing" in the early stages of a relationship. They shower their partner with excessive attention, compliments, and gifts to create a sense of dependency and control.

5. **Boundary violations**: Watch out for individuals who consistently disregard your boundaries and personal space. They may invade your privacy, make decisions for you without your consent, or pressure you into doing things you're uncomfortable with.

Variations in Severity and Presentations

It's important to note that narcissistic personality styles can vary in severity and presentation. Some individuals may exhibit more covert narcissistic traits, while others may display more overt narcissistic traits. Covert narcissists tend to be more introverted and may mask their grandiosity and need for admiration behind a facade of humility and selflessness. Overt narcissists, on the other hand, are more obvious in their self-centeredness and may openly seek attention and admiration.

Additionally, narcissistic traits can manifest differently in males, females, and within the GLBTQI community. Societal expectations and stereotypes can influence the way narcissism is expressed and perceived in different genders and sexual orientations. It's important to recognize that narcissism is not limited to any specific gender or sexual orientation, and anyone can exhibit narcissistic traits.

Conclusion

When it comes to dating and narcissistic personality styles, it's crucial to be aware of the red flags and potential warning signs. By recognizing these traits early on, you can make more informed decisions about whether to pursue a relationship with someone who exhibits narcissistic tendencies. Remember, it's not your fault if you find yourself in a relationship with a narcissist, as many people have experienced similar situations. In the next chapter, we will explore strategies for understanding and surviving relationships with narcissists, as well as looking after yourself and healing after the relationship ends.

2.3 Understanding and Surviving Relationships with Narcissists

Navigating relationships with narcissists can be challenging and emotionally draining. Whether it's a romantic partner, family member, boss, or friend, understanding and surviving these relationships requires knowledge, self-awareness, and effective coping strategies. In this chapter, we will explore the dynamics of relationships with narcissists, provide insights into their behaviors, and offer guidance on how to protect yourself and maintain your well-being.

2.3.1 Recognizing Narcissistic Behaviors

Before delving into strategies for surviving relationships with narcissists, it is crucial to understand the traits and behaviors associated with narcissistic personality styles. Narcissists often exhibit a sense of entitlement, an excessive need for admiration, and a lack of empathy. They may manipulate others to meet their own needs, engage in grandiose self-promotion, and have a fragile self-esteem that is easily threatened.

Narcissistic behaviors can manifest in two primary styles: covert and overt. Covert narcissists are often characterized by their subtle manipulation tactics, passive-aggressive behavior, and a facade of humility. They may appear charming and empathetic on the surface but use covert tactics to control and manipulate others. Overt narcissists, on the other hand, display their grandiosity and self-importance openly. They seek constant attention and admiration, often dominating conversations and belittling others to boost their own ego.

It is important to note that narcissistic personality styles exist on a spectrum, with variations in severity and presentations. Some individuals may exhibit only a few narcissistic traits, while others may display a full-blown narcissistic personality disorder. Understanding these variations can help you gauge the level of toxicity in your relationship and determine the best course of action.

2.3.2 Red Flags in Romantic Relationships

When it comes to romantic relationships, it is essential to be aware of the red flags that may indicate a potential narcissistic partner. While not all individuals who display these traits are narcissists, they can serve as warning signs to proceed with caution. Some common red flags include:

1. Excessive self-centeredness: A narcissistic partner may consistently prioritize their own needs and desires over yours, showing little regard for your feelings or opinions.
2. Lack of empathy: They may struggle to understand or validate your emotions, often dismissing or minimizing them.
3. Manipulative behavior: Narcissists are skilled at manipulating others to get what they want. They may use guilt, gaslighting, or emotional blackmail to control and dominate the relationship.
4. Grandiose self-image: Pay attention to excessive bragging, a sense of entitlement, and an inflated sense of self-importance.
5. Lack of accountability: Narcissists often deflect blame onto others and refuse to take responsibility for their actions or mistakes.
6. Love-bombing followed by devaluation: In the early stages of the

relationship, a narcissistic partner may shower you with affection and attention. However, this can quickly turn into devaluation, where they criticize, belittle, or emotionally abuse you.

2.3.3 Coping Strategies for Surviving Relationships with Narcissists

Surviving relationships with narcissists requires a combination of self-care, boundary-setting, and effective communication. Here are some strategies to help you navigate these challenging dynamics:

1. Establish and maintain boundaries: Clearly define your limits and communicate them assertively. Narcissists may push boundaries, so it is crucial to stay firm and consistent in enforcing them.
2. Practice self-care: Prioritize your emotional well-being by engaging in activities that bring you joy and relaxation. Surround yourself with a support network of trusted friends and family who can provide validation and understanding.
3. Develop a support system: Seek therapy or support groups to gain insight into narcissistic behaviors and receive guidance on coping strategies. Connecting with others who have experienced similar relationships can be empowering and validating.
4. Focus on your self-worth: Remind yourself of your value and worthiness outside of the relationship. Engage in self-reflection and challenge any negative beliefs or self-blame that may have developed during the relationship.
5. Limit contact and exposure: If possible, minimize contact with the narcissistic individual to protect your emotional well-being. This may involve setting boundaries around communication or even considering ending the relationship if it becomes toxic and harmful.
6. Seek professional help if necessary: If the relationship becomes emotionally or physically abusive, it is crucial to prioritize your safety. Reach out to professionals, such as therapists or counselors, who can guide you through the process of leaving and healing from the relationship.

Remember, surviving a relationship with a narcissist is not easy, and it is important to be patient and compassionate with yourself. Healing takes time, and it is essential to acknowledge that you are not to blame for the narcissist's behavior. Many individuals have experienced relationships with narcissists, and with the right support and strategies, you can move forward and rebuild a healthier, more fulfilling life.

2.4 Looking After Yourself

When it comes to dealing with narcissistic personality styles, it is crucial to prioritize your own well-being and take steps to protect yourself from further harm. This section will provide you with valuable insights and strategies to help you heal and move on from a relationship with a narcissist. Remember, you are not alone in this journey, and many individuals have experienced similar challenges.

2.4.1 Recognizing the Impact of Narcissistic Abuse

Before delving into the healing process, it is important to acknowledge the impact that narcissistic abuse can have on your mental, emotional, and physical well-being. Narcissists are skilled manipulators who use various tactics to control and demean their victims. Gaslighting, emotional manipulation, and constant criticism can leave you feeling confused, anxious, and depleted.

It is common for victims of narcissistic abuse to blame themselves for the deterioration of the relationship. However, it is crucial to understand that the narcissist's behavior is not your fault. Narcissists have deep-seated issues that stem from their own insecurities and lack of empathy. By recognizing this, you can begin to shift the blame away from yourself and focus on your own healing.

2.4.2 Seeking Support and Building a Support Network

Recovering from a relationship with a narcissist can be a challenging and emotional process. It is important to seek support from trusted friends, family members, or professionals who can provide guidance and understanding. Surrounding yourself with a supportive network can help validate your experiences and provide a safe space for you to heal.

Consider reaching out to support groups or online communities where you can connect with others who have gone through similar experiences. Sharing your story and listening to the stories of others can be incredibly empowering and help you realize that you are not alone.

2.4.3 Rebuilding Self-Esteem and Self-Worth

One of the most damaging effects of being in a relationship with a narcissist is the erosion of your self-esteem and self-worth. Narcissists often belittle and devalue their partners, leaving them feeling unworthy and inadequate. Rebuilding your self-esteem is a crucial step in the healing process.

Start by practicing self-care and self-compassion. Engage in activities that bring you joy and make you feel good about yourself. Surround yourself with positive influences and affirmations. Challenge negative self-talk and replace it with positive and empowering thoughts.

Therapy can also be immensely helpful in rebuilding your self-esteem. A trained therapist can guide you through the healing process, help you identify and challenge negative beliefs, and provide you with tools to rebuild your self-worth.

2.4.4 Setting Healthy Boundaries and Trusting Again

After experiencing a relationship with a narcissist, it is common to have difficulty trusting others. However, it is important to remember that not everyone is a narcissist, and healthy relationships are possible.

Setting healthy boundaries is crucial in protecting yourself from future harm. Learn to recognize and assert your needs and desires. Communicate your boundaries clearly and firmly, and be prepared to enforce them if they are crossed. Surround yourself with individuals who respect and value your boundaries.

Take your time when entering into new relationships. Be cautious and observant of any red flags that may indicate narcissistic traits in a potential partner. Trust your instincts and prioritize your own well-being above all else.

2.4.5 Practicing Self-Care and Nurturing Your Emotional Well-being

Self-care is an essential aspect of healing and moving on from a relationship with a narcissist. Make self-care a priority in your life by engaging in activities that promote your emotional well-being. This can include practicing mindfulness, engaging in hobbies, spending time in nature, or seeking professional help when needed.

Nurture your emotional well-being by surrounding yourself with positive influences and engaging in activities that bring you joy and fulfillment. Focus on self-love and self-compassion, and remind yourself that you deserve happiness and a healthy, fulfilling life.

Remember, healing takes time, and everyone's journey is unique. Be patient with yourself and celebrate even the smallest victories along the way. You have the strength and resilience to overcome the challenges of a relationship with a narcissist and create a life filled with authenticity, fulfillment, and healthy relationships.

3

Chapter 3

Narcissism Beyond Romantic Relationships

3.1 Managing Narcissistic Relatives

Dealing with narcissistic relatives can be a challenging and emotionally draining experience. Whether it's a parent, sibling, or extended family member, the presence of narcissistic traits can significantly impact your well-being and relationships. In this section, we will explore strategies for self-preservation when managing narcissistic relatives.

Understanding Narcissistic Relatives

Narcissistic relatives exhibit similar traits to those with Narcissistic Personality Disorder (NPD). They have an inflated sense of self-importance, a constant need for admiration, and a lack of empathy for others. However, it's important to note that not all narcissistic relatives have a diagnosable personality disorder. Some may display covert narcissism, characterized by subtle manipulation and a victim mentality, while others may exhibit overt narcissism, which is more obvious and grandiose in nature.

Setting Boundaries

When dealing with narcissistic relatives, setting and maintaining boundaries is crucial for your emotional well-being. Establishing clear limits on what you will and will not tolerate can help protect yourself from their manipulative tactics. Communicate your boundaries assertively and consistently, making it clear that you expect respect and healthy interactions.

Limiting Contact

In some cases, limiting contact with narcissistic relatives may be necessary for your own mental health. This can involve reducing the frequency of interactions or even cutting off contact entirely. While this decision may be difficult, it is essential to prioritize your well-being and surround yourself with positive influences.

Managing Expectations

It's important to recognize that you cannot change or fix a narcissistic relative. Accepting this reality can help you manage your expectations and avoid unnecessary disappointment. Instead, focus on taking care of yourself and finding healthy outlets for support and validation.

Seeking Support

Dealing with narcissistic relatives can be isolating, as they often manipulate and gaslight their loved ones. It is crucial to seek support from trusted friends, therapists, or support groups who can provide validation and guidance. Sharing your experiences with others who have dealt with similar situations can be incredibly empowering and help you navigate the challenges more effectively.

Developing Emotional Resilience

Building emotional resilience is key to managing narcissistic relatives. This involves developing self-awareness, practicing self-care, and cultivating a strong support network. Engaging in activities that bring you joy, practicing mindfulness, and seeking therapy can all contribute to your emotional well-being and resilience.

Navigating Family Gatherings

Family gatherings can be particularly challenging when dealing with narcissistic relatives. It's important to prepare yourself mentally and emotionally before attending such events. Remind yourself of your boundaries and practice self-care strategies to help you stay grounded and maintain your emotional well-being.

Protecting Children

If you have children, it is crucial to shield them from the negative influence of narcissistic relatives. Establish clear boundaries regarding their interactions with your children and educate them about healthy relationships. Encourage open communication and provide a safe space for them to express their feelings and concerns.

Seeking Professional Help

In some cases, the impact of dealing with narcissistic relatives may require professional intervention. A therapist or counselor can provide guidance, support, and strategies for managing the challenges associated with these relationships. They can also help you navigate the complex emotions that arise from dealing with narcissistic relatives.

Remember, managing narcissistic relatives is a continuous process that requires self-care, self-compassion, and a commitment to your own well-being. By setting boundaries, seeking support, and prioritizing your emotional health, you can navigate these challenging relationships with greater resilience and self-preservation.

3.2 Navigating Narcissistic Bosses

Dealing with a narcissistic boss can be a challenging and emotionally draining experience. Narcissistic personality styles in the workplace can manifest in various ways, making it important to understand how to navigate these situations effectively. In this section, we will explore strategies for coping with narcissistic bosses and maintaining your well-being in the workplace.

Understanding Narcissistic Bosses

Narcissistic bosses exhibit a range of traits that can make working with them difficult. They often have an inflated sense of self-importance, a constant need for admiration, and a lack of empathy towards others. These individuals may prioritize their own success and image above the well-being of their employees, leading to a toxic work environment.

Narcissistic bosses may engage in manipulative behaviors such as gaslighting, where they distort reality to make you doubt your own perceptions and abilities. They may also engage in favoritism, pitting employees against each other to maintain control and power. It is important to recognize these behaviors and understand that they stem from the narcissistic boss's own insecurities and need for control.

Coping Strategies

1. **Maintain Professionalism**: When dealing with a narcissistic boss, it is crucial to remain professional and composed. Avoid reacting emotionally to their provocations or engaging in power struggles. Instead, focus on your work and strive to meet their expectations to the

best of your abilities.

2. **Set Boundaries**: Establish clear boundaries with your narcissistic boss to protect your well-being. Clearly communicate your limits and expectations, and assertively express your needs. This can help prevent them from taking advantage of you or crossing personal boundaries.

3. **Document Everything**: Keep a record of your interactions with your boss, including emails, memos, and meeting minutes. This documentation can serve as evidence in case you need to address any issues or defend yourself against false accusations.

4. **Seek Support**: Find a trusted colleague or mentor who can provide guidance and support during challenging situations. Having someone to confide in can help you navigate the difficulties of working with a narcissistic boss and provide a sense of validation.

5. **Focus on Self-Care**: It is essential to prioritize self-care when dealing with a narcissistic boss. Engage in activities that help you relax and recharge outside of work. Practice stress management techniques such as mindfulness, exercise, and maintaining a healthy work-life balance.

6. **Develop Emotional Resilience**: Building emotional resilience can help you cope with the emotional toll of working with a narcissistic boss. This involves developing self-awareness, cultivating a positive mindset, and learning to detach emotionally from their manipulative tactics.

7. **Seek Opportunities for Growth**: Despite the challenges, try to find opportunities for personal and professional growth within your role. Focus on developing your skills and expanding your network, which can provide you with options for advancement or alternative job opportunities in the future.

Dealing with Specific Situations

1. **Handling Criticism**: Narcissistic bosses often criticize and belittle their employees to maintain control. When faced with criticism, remain calm and objective. Evaluate the validity of the feedback and address

any legitimate concerns while disregarding any unfounded attacks on your abilities.

2. **Managing Micromanagement**: Narcissistic bosses may have a strong need for control and may micromanage their employees. To cope with this, ensure clear communication and provide regular updates on your progress. This can help alleviate their need for constant supervision and demonstrate your competence.

3. **Navigating Office Politics**: Narcissistic bosses may create a toxic work environment by fostering office politics and favoritism. Avoid getting involved in gossip or taking sides. Focus on building positive relationships with your colleagues based on professionalism and mutual respect.

4. **Seeking External Support**: If the situation becomes unbearable, consider seeking support from Human Resources or higher management. Present your concerns in a calm and factual manner, providing evidence if necessary. However, be aware that not all organizations may be equipped to handle such situations effectively.

Remember, it is essential to prioritize your well-being and mental health when dealing with a narcissistic boss. Recognize that their behavior is a reflection of their own insecurities and not a reflection of your worth or abilities. By implementing these coping strategies, you can navigate the challenges of working with a narcissistic boss while maintaining your own personal and professional growth.

3.3 Maintaining Boundaries with Narcissistic Friends

Maintaining healthy boundaries is crucial when dealing with narcissistic friends. While it may be challenging to recognize the signs of narcissism in friendships, it is essential to protect your emotional well-being and maintain a sense of self. In this section, we will explore strategies for setting boundaries, identifying red flags, and navigating friendships with narcissistic individuals.

Recognizing Narcissistic Friends

Identifying narcissistic traits in friends can be more difficult than in romantic relationships or professional settings. Friends often have a history together, making it harder to notice subtle changes in behavior. However, there are several red flags to watch out for:

1. **Excessive need for attention**: Narcissistic friends often dominate conversations, constantly seeking validation and admiration from others. They may interrupt or dismiss your thoughts and feelings, redirecting the conversation back to themselves.
2. **Lack of empathy**: Narcissistic friends struggle to empathize with others and may dismiss or invalidate your emotions. They may only show interest in your life when it benefits them or when they can use it to their advantage.
3. **Manipulative behavior**: Narcissistic friends may use manipulation tactics to control and manipulate you. They may guilt-trip, gaslight, or exploit your vulnerabilities to get what they want.
4. **Sense of entitlement**: Narcissistic friends believe they are superior and entitled to special treatment. They may expect you to cater to their needs and desires without reciprocating.
5. **Constant need for admiration**: Narcissistic friends crave constant praise and admiration. They may fish for compliments, exaggerate their achievements, or belittle others to boost their own ego.

Setting Boundaries

Establishing and maintaining boundaries is crucial when dealing with narcissistic friends. Here are some strategies to help you maintain your emotional well-being:

1. **Identify your limits**: Reflect on your values, needs, and personal boundaries. Understand what you are comfortable with and what

crosses the line for you. This self-awareness will help you establish clear boundaries.

2. **Communicate assertively**: Clearly and assertively communicate your boundaries to your narcissistic friend. Use "I" statements to express how their behavior affects you and what you need from the friendship. Be prepared for resistance or defensiveness, but stand firm in your boundaries.

3. **Limit your availability**: Set limits on the time and energy you invest in the friendship. Avoid being available at their beck and call and prioritize your own needs and well-being.

4. **Practice self-care**: Engage in activities that bring you joy and fulfillment outside of the friendship. Nurture your own emotional well-being by focusing on self-care, hobbies, and spending time with supportive individuals.

5. **Seek support**: Reach out to trusted friends, family members, or a therapist who can provide guidance and support. Having a support system can help you navigate the challenges of maintaining boundaries with a narcissistic friend.

Navigating the Friendship

Navigating a friendship with a narcissistic individual requires careful consideration and self-protection. Here are some additional strategies to help you maintain your well-being:

1. **Manage your expectations**: Understand that you cannot change or fix a narcissistic friend. Accepting this reality will help you set realistic expectations for the friendship and avoid disappointment.

2. **Avoid engaging in power struggles**: Narcissistic friends thrive on power and control. Refrain from engaging in arguments or power struggles, as it will only fuel their need for attention and validation.

3. **Practice detachment**: Emotionally detach yourself from their manipulative tactics and focus on your own well-being. Remind yourself

that their behavior is a reflection of their own insecurities and not a reflection of your worth.

4. **Maintain a support network**: Surround yourself with supportive friends who understand your situation. Having a strong support network will provide you with validation, empathy, and guidance when dealing with the challenges of a narcissistic friendship.

5. **Consider ending the friendship**: If the friendship becomes toxic and consistently undermines your well-being, it may be necessary to consider ending the relationship. Prioritize your mental and emotional health above maintaining a toxic friendship.

Remember, maintaining boundaries with narcissistic friends can be challenging, but it is essential for your well-being. By recognizing the red flags, setting clear boundaries, and prioritizing self-care, you can navigate these friendships with greater confidence and protect your emotional health.

3.4 Narcissism in the GLBTQI Community

Narcissism is a complex personality style that can manifest in various ways within different communities and social contexts. In this chapter, we will explore the unique challenges and perspectives of narcissism within the GLBTQI (gay, lesbian, bisexual, transgender, intersex, and queer) community. We will discuss the specific traits and behaviors to look out for, as well as strategies for supporting GLBTQI individuals who have been affected by narcissistic abuse.

3.4.1 Understanding Narcissistic Traits in GLBTQI Relationships

Narcissistic traits can be observed in individuals across all sexual orientations and gender identities, including within the GLBTQI community. It is important to note that narcissism is not exclusive to any particular group, but rather a personality style that can be found in individuals from all walks of life.

In GLBTQI relationships, narcissistic traits may present themselves in various ways. For example, a narcissistic partner may exhibit a sense of entitlement, a need for constant admiration, and a lack of empathy towards their partner's feelings and experiences. They may also engage in manipulative behaviors, such as gaslighting, to maintain control and power over their partner.

It is crucial to recognize these traits early on in a relationship to avoid potential harm and emotional abuse. Some red flags to look out for include:

1. Excessive self-centeredness: A narcissistic partner may consistently prioritize their own needs and desires over their partner's, showing little regard for their feelings or well-being.
2. Lack of empathy: They may struggle to understand or validate their partner's emotions, dismissing or minimizing their experiences.
3. Grandiose sense of self-importance: Narcissistic individuals often have an inflated sense of their own achievements and abilities, seeking constant validation and admiration from others.
4. Manipulative behavior: They may use tactics such as gaslighting, where they distort or deny their partner's reality, making them question their own perceptions and sanity.
5. Lack of accountability: Narcissists often refuse to take responsibility for their actions, shifting blame onto their partner or external factors.

3.4.2 Supporting GLBTQI Victims of Narcissistic Abuse

GLBTQI individuals who have experienced narcissistic abuse may face unique challenges due to societal attitudes, discrimination, and the intersectionality of their identities. It is essential to provide support and understanding to those who have been affected by narcissistic partners within the GLBTQI community.

1. Creating safe spaces: Establishing supportive environments where GLBTQI individuals can share their experiences and seek guidance is

crucial. This can be done through support groups, online communities, or counseling services specifically tailored to the GLBTQI community.

2. Encouraging self-compassion: Victims of narcissistic abuse often blame themselves for the toxic dynamics in their relationships. It is important to emphasize that no one deserves to be mistreated and to help survivors develop self-compassion and self-forgiveness.

3. Promoting self-care: Encouraging self-care practices, such as engaging in hobbies, seeking therapy, and practicing mindfulness, can help survivors of narcissistic abuse rebuild their emotional well-being and regain a sense of self.

4. Addressing intersectionality: Recognizing the unique challenges faced by GLBTQI individuals who have experienced narcissistic abuse is crucial. Understanding the intersectionality of their identities and providing support that is inclusive and sensitive to their specific needs is essential.

3.4.3 Building Healthy Relationships within the GLBTQI Community

While it is important to be aware of the signs of narcissism and protect oneself from potential harm, it is equally important to foster healthy relationships within the GLBTQI community. Here are some strategies for building and maintaining healthy relationships:

1. Self-awareness: Developing self-awareness and understanding one's own needs, boundaries, and values is essential in establishing healthy relationships. This self-awareness can help individuals recognize and avoid potential narcissistic partners.

2. Communication and consent: Open and honest communication, along with mutual respect for boundaries and consent, are the foundations of healthy relationships. It is important to establish clear expectations and maintain ongoing dialogue with partners.

3. Supportive networks: Surrounding oneself with a supportive network

of friends, family, and community members can provide a sense of belonging and emotional support. These networks can also serve as a source of guidance and validation in navigating relationships.

4. Seeking professional help: If past experiences with narcissistic partners have left emotional scars, seeking therapy or counseling can be beneficial. A mental health professional can provide guidance and support in healing from past trauma and developing healthy relationship patterns.

By understanding the unique challenges and perspectives of narcissism within the GLBTQI community, we can better support individuals who have been affected by narcissistic abuse. Building healthy relationships and fostering a sense of community can empower GLBTQI individuals to thrive and overcome the negative impacts of narcissistic personality styles.

4

Chapter 4

Understanding the Impact of Narcissistic Personality Styles

4.1 The Emotional Toll

Living and interacting with individuals who exhibit narcissistic personality styles can have a profound impact on one's mental and emotional well-being. The emotional toll of being in a relationship with a narcissist is often underestimated, as the manipulative tactics and self-centered behavior can leave lasting scars on the victim's psyche. In this section, we will explore the various ways in which narcissistic personality styles can affect an individual's mental and emotional well-being.

4.1.1 The Manipulative Power of Narcissists

Narcissists possess a unique ability to manipulate and control others for their own gain. They often employ tactics such as gaslighting, where they distort reality and make the victim doubt their own perceptions and memories. Gaslighting can lead to confusion, self-doubt, and a loss of trust in oneself. Other manipulative tactics include projection, where the narcissist blames others for their own shortcomings, and triangulation, where they create conflicts between individuals to maintain control.

4.1.2 Emotional Abuse and Trauma

Being in a relationship with a narcissist can result in emotional abuse and trauma. The constant criticism, belittling, and demeaning behavior can erode the victim's self-esteem and self-worth. The emotional abuse inflicted by narcissists can leave deep emotional scars that may take years to heal. Victims often experience feelings of worthlessness, anxiety, depression, and a loss of identity.

4.1.3 Lack of Emotional Connection

One of the defining traits of narcissistic personality styles is the lack of empathy and emotional connection. Narcissists are unable to genuinely connect with others on an emotional level, as they are primarily focused on their own needs and desires. This lack of emotional connection can leave the victim feeling isolated, unimportant, and emotionally neglected.

4.1.4 Self-Blame and Internalization

Victims of narcissistic abuse often blame themselves for the toxic dynamics in the relationship. The narcissist's manipulative tactics can make the victim question their own worth and sanity. It is important to understand that the emotional toll of being in a relationship with a narcissist is not the victim's fault. It is a result of the narcissist's distorted perception of reality and their need for power and control.

4.1.5 Variations in Severity and Presentations

Narcissistic personality styles can vary in severity and presentations. Some individuals may exhibit overt narcissism, where their grandiosity and self-importance are readily apparent. Others may display covert narcissism, where their narcissistic traits are hidden beneath a facade of humility and victimhood. Understanding these variations is crucial in recognizing and dealing with narcissistic individuals in different contexts.

4.1.6 Impact on Mental and Emotional Well-being

The emotional toll of narcissistic personality styles can have a significant impact on an individual's mental and emotional well-being. Victims may experience symptoms of anxiety, depression, post-traumatic stress disorder (PTSD), and complex trauma. It is important for individuals who have been in relationships with narcissists to seek professional help and support to address the emotional wounds and regain their sense of self.

4.1.7 Healing and Recovery

Recovering from the emotional toll of narcissistic abuse requires time, self-compassion, and support. It is essential for victims to recognize that they are not alone and that many others have experienced similar challenges. Seeking therapy, joining support groups, and practicing self-care are crucial steps in the healing process. Rebuilding self-esteem, setting healthy boundaries, and learning to trust again are essential components of the recovery journey.

4.1.8 Moving Forward: Setting Healthy Boundaries

Moving forward after narcissistic abuse involves setting and maintaining healthy boundaries. Victims must learn to prioritize their own well-being and protect themselves from further harm. This includes learning to say no, asserting one's needs and desires, and surrounding oneself with supportive and empathetic individuals.

4.1.9 Avoiding Narcissistic Relationships

Prevention is key in avoiding future involvement in narcissistic relationships. Learning to identify early warning signs and red flags is crucial in protecting oneself from potential narcissistic partners. Developing healthy relationship patterns, such as effective communication, mutual respect, and shared values, can help individuals avoid falling into the trap of narcissistic relationships.

In conclusion, the emotional toll of narcissistic personality styles is significant and can have long-lasting effects on an individual's mental and emotional well-being. Recognizing the manipulative tactics, understanding the lack of emotional connection, and seeking support are essential steps in healing and recovering from narcissistic abuse. By setting healthy boundaries and avoiding narcissistic relationships, individuals can empower themselves and create a life free from the emotional turmoil inflicted by narcissistic individuals.

4.2 The Psychological Manipulation

Narcissistic personality styles are characterized by a range of manipulative tactics that individuals with this disorder employ to control and dominate others. These tactics can be both overt and covert, and they are designed to exploit and manipulate the emotions and vulnerabilities of their victims. Understanding these psychological manipulation techniques is crucial in recognizing and protecting oneself from the harmful effects of narcissistic abuse.

4.2.1 Gaslighting: The Art of Distorting Reality

Gaslighting is one of the most insidious and damaging manipulation tactics employed by narcissists. It involves the deliberate distortion of reality to make the victim doubt their own perceptions, memories, and sanity. Gaslighting can take various forms, such as denying events that occurred, rewriting history, or even directly contradicting the victim's experiences.

The goal of gaslighting is to gain control over the victim by making them question their own reality and rely on the narcissist's version of events.

Gaslighting can be extremely damaging to the victim's self-esteem and mental well-being. It erodes their sense of self and creates a state of confusion and self-doubt. Victims of gaslighting often find themselves constantly questioning their own judgment and feeling like they are going crazy. Recognizing gaslighting is the first step in breaking free from the narcissist's control.

4.2.2 Manipulative Charm: The Mask of the Narcissist

Narcissists are often skilled at presenting a charming and charismatic facade to the outside world. They can be incredibly charming, charismatic, and persuasive, which makes it difficult for others to see through their manipulative tactics. This charm is often used as a tool to manipulate and exploit others for their own gain.

The narcissist's charm is not genuine but rather a calculated strategy to win over their victims. They use flattery, compliments, and grand gestures to create a sense of admiration and dependency in their targets. This charm can be particularly enticing in the early stages of a romantic relationship, where the narcissist may appear to be the perfect partner. However, it is important to remain vigilant and not be swayed solely by their charm, as it is often a mask hiding their true intentions.

4.2.3 Emotional Manipulation: Playing with Your Feelings

Narcissists are masters of emotional manipulation. They have an uncanny ability to identify and exploit their victim's vulnerabilities, using them to gain control and power. Emotional manipulation can take many forms, including guilt-tripping, playing the victim, and using emotional blackmail.

Guilt-tripping is a common tactic used by narcissists to make their victims feel responsible for their negative emotions or actions. They may use phrases like "If you really loved me, you would..." or "You're the only one who can make me happy." By placing the blame on their victims, narcissists manipulate them into feeling guilty and responsible for the narcissist's emotional well-being.

Playing the victim is another manipulation tactic employed by narcissists. They often portray themselves as the innocent party, unfairly treated by others. This tactic is used to gain sympathy and support from others, while deflecting attention away from their own harmful behavior.

Emotional blackmail is a particularly damaging form of manipulation. Narcissists may threaten to withhold love, affection, or support unless their demands are met. This manipulation tactic can leave the victim feeling trapped and powerless, as they fear losing the narcissist's love and approval.

4.2.4 Triangulation: Divide and Conquer

Triangulation is a manipulation tactic used by narcissists to create conflict and competition among their victims. It involves bringing a third party into the relationship dynamic, often by forming alliances or seeking validation from others. By triangulating their victims, narcissists create a sense of rivalry and insecurity, which further strengthens their control over the situation.

Triangulation can take various forms, such as comparing one victim to another, spreading rumors or gossip, or seeking attention and validation from others to make their victims feel inadequate. This manipulation tactic serves to keep the victims off-balance and constantly striving for the narcissist's approval.

4.2.5 Hoovering: The Cycle of Abuse

Hoovering is a manipulation tactic employed by narcissists to draw their victims back into the abusive relationship. It is named after the vacuum cleaner brand Hoover, as it refers to the narcissist's attempt to suck their victims back into their orbit. Hoovering often occurs after a period of no contact or when the victim is attempting to move on from the relationship.

Narcissists use hoovering as a way to regain control and power over their victims. They may employ various tactics, such as love bombing, promises of change, or threats and intimidation, to lure their victims back into the relationship. Hoovering can be incredibly difficult to resist, as the narcissist knows exactly how to exploit the victim's vulnerabilities and emotional attachments.

Recognizing hoovering for what it is and maintaining strong boundaries is essential in breaking free from the cycle of abuse and moving towards healing and recovery.

4.2.6 The Impact of Psychological Manipulation

The psychological manipulation tactics employed by narcissists can have severe and long-lasting effects on their victims. Gaslighting, emotional manipulation, and other tactics can lead to a range of emotional and psychological consequences, including low self-esteem, anxiety, depression, and post-traumatic stress disorder (PTSD).

It is important to understand that the manipulation tactics used by narcissists are not a reflection of the victim's worth or intelligence. Victims of narcissistic abuse often blame themselves for the abuse, believing that they should have seen the signs or been able to prevent it. However, it is crucial to remember that narcissists are skilled manipulators who prey on the vulnerabilities of others.

By gaining an understanding of the psychological manipulation tactics employed by narcissists, individuals can begin to recognize and protect themselves from these harmful behaviors. Building a support network, seeking therapy, and practicing self-care are essential steps in healing and recovering from the effects of narcissistic abuse. Remember, you are not alone, and there is hope for a brighter future beyond the grasp of narcissistic personality styles.

4.3 The Societal Impact

Narcissism, in its various forms, has always existed within society. However, with the advent of the digital age, the impact of narcissistic personality styles has become more pronounced and far-reaching. The rise of social media platforms and the constant need for validation and attention have created a breeding ground for narcissistic behaviors to thrive. In this section, we will explore the societal impact of narcissism in the digital age and how it affects individuals and communities.

4.3.1 The Rise of the Digital Narcissist

The digital age has provided a platform for individuals with narcissistic personality styles to amplify their behaviors and seek constant validation. Social media platforms, such as Facebook, Instagram, and Twitter, have become virtual mirrors for narcissists to showcase their idealized self-image and garner admiration from others. The ability to curate and control their online persona allows narcissists to manipulate their image and project a false sense of superiority.

4.3.2 The Illusion of Connection

While social media has made it easier for people to connect with others, it has also created a superficial sense of connection that feeds into narcissistic tendencies. Likes, comments, and followers have become the currency of validation, and narcissists thrive on the attention and admiration they receive. However, these connections are often shallow and lack the depth and authenticity that comes with genuine human interaction.

4.3.3 The Impact on Mental Health

The constant exposure to carefully curated online personas can have a detrimental effect on the mental health of individuals. Comparing oneself to the seemingly perfect lives of others can lead to feelings of inadequacy, low self-esteem, and depression. The pressure to maintain a flawless online image can also contribute to anxiety and stress. Additionally, the constant need for validation and attention can create a cycle of dependency on external sources for self-worth, further exacerbating the negative impact on mental health.

4.3.4 The Erosion of Empathy

Narcissistic personality styles are characterized by a lack of empathy and an inability to connect emotionally with others. The digital age has further perpetuated this empathy deficit by creating a culture of self-centeredness and instant gratification. Online interactions often lack the nuances of face-to-face communication, making it easier for narcissists to disregard the feelings and needs of others. This erosion of empathy can have far-reaching consequences, not only on individual relationships but also on the fabric of society as a whole.

4.3.5 The Spread of Narcissistic Behaviors

The digital age has also facilitated the spread of narcissistic behaviors and attitudes. The constant exposure to narcissistic individuals and their behaviors can normalize and even encourage such traits in others. This can lead to a society that values self-promotion, entitlement, and a lack of consideration for others. The prevalence of narcissistic behaviors can have a detrimental effect on the overall well-being and functioning of communities, as cooperation and empathy are replaced by self-interest and manipulation.

4.3.6 Navigating the Digital Landscape

In order to navigate the digital landscape and protect ourselves from the negative impact of narcissistic personality styles, it is important to be aware of the red flags and warning signs. Understanding the tactics used by narcissists, such as grandiosity, manipulation, and gaslighting, can help us identify and avoid getting involved in toxic relationships, both online and offline. It is crucial to prioritize our mental and emotional well-being by setting boundaries, practicing self-care, and seeking support when needed.

4.3.7 Promoting Healthy Digital Relationships

While the digital age has its challenges, it also presents opportunities for positive change. By promoting healthy digital relationships, we can counteract the negative impact of narcissistic behaviors. This involves fostering empathy, kindness, and authenticity in our online interactions. By supporting and uplifting others, we can create a virtual community that values genuine connections and promotes emotional well-being.

In conclusion, the societal impact of narcissistic personality styles in the digital age is significant and far-reaching. The rise of the digital narcissist, the illusion of connection, the impact on mental health, the erosion of empathy, and the spread of narcissistic behaviors all contribute to a culture that values self-promotion and self-interest over genuine human connection. However, by being aware of the red flags, setting boundaries, and promoting healthy digital relationships, we can protect ourselves and create a more empathetic and authentic online community.

4.4 The Empathy Deficit: Understanding the Lack of Emotional Connection

Narcissistic personality styles are characterized by a profound lack of empathy and an excessive preoccupation with oneself. This lack of empathy is a core feature of narcissism and is often one of the most challenging aspects to navigate when dealing with individuals who exhibit narcissistic traits. In this section, we will explore the empathy deficit commonly found in narcissistic personality styles and its impact on relationships and interactions.

4.4.1 The Nature of Empathy

Empathy is the ability to understand and share the feelings of others. It involves being able to put oneself in another person's shoes, to recognize and validate their emotions, and to respond with compassion and understanding. Empathy is a fundamental aspect of healthy social interactions and is crucial for building and maintaining meaningful relationships.

4.4.2 The Lack of Emotional Connection

One of the defining characteristics of narcissistic personality styles is the inability to form genuine emotional connections with others. Narcissists often struggle to understand and relate to the emotions and experiences of those around them. They may appear indifferent or dismissive of others' feelings, focusing instead on their own needs and desires.

This lack of emotional connection can manifest in various ways. For example, narcissists may struggle to show genuine concern or empathy when someone is going through a difficult time. They may minimize or invalidate others' emotions, viewing them as insignificant compared to their own. This emotional disconnect can leave those in relationships with narcissists feeling unheard, unseen, and emotionally neglected.

4.4.3 The Self-Centered Focus

Narcissistic personality styles are characterized by an excessive preoccupation with oneself. Narcissists often prioritize their own needs, desires, and achievements above all else. This self-centered focus leaves little room for considering the feelings and experiences of others.

Narcissists may struggle to recognize or acknowledge the impact of their behavior on those around them. They may be oblivious to the hurt or distress they cause, as their primary concern is their own gratification and self-image. This self-centeredness can make it challenging for narcissists to engage in meaningful and empathetic interactions with others.

4.4.4 Covert Narcissism and Empathy

Covert narcissism refers to a subtype of narcissistic personality style characterized by a more subtle and hidden expression of narcissistic traits. While overt narcissists may display their self-centeredness more openly, covert narcissists often mask their narcissistic tendencies behind a facade of humility or selflessness.

Despite their outward appearance of empathy and concern for others, covert narcissists still struggle with a genuine emotional connection. Their empathy deficit may be more difficult to detect, as they may appear caring and compassionate on the surface. However, their underlying motivations are often driven by a need for validation and admiration rather than a genuine concern for others' well-being.

4.4.5 Overt Narcissism and Empathy

Overt narcissism, on the other hand, is characterized by a more overt and grandiose expression of narcissistic traits. Overt narcissists often display a sense of entitlement, arrogance, and a lack of regard for others' feelings. They may dominate conversations, dismiss others' opinions, and seek constant admiration and attention.

The lack of empathy in overt narcissists is often more apparent, as they may openly disregard or belittle others' emotions. They may exploit and manipulate others for their own gain, showing little remorse or consideration for the harm they cause. Their self-centeredness and grandiosity can make it challenging for them to connect with others on an emotional level.

4.4.6 Variations in Severity and Presentations

Narcissistic personality styles can vary in severity and presentations. Some individuals may exhibit only a few narcissistic traits, while others may display a more pervasive pattern of narcissistic behavior. The severity of narcissism can impact the degree to which individuals struggle with empathy and emotional connection.

In some cases, individuals with narcissistic traits may be capable of displaying empathy in certain situations or with certain individuals. However, this empathy is often conditional and driven by self-interest. They may only show empathy when it serves their own needs or when they can gain something from it.

4.4.7 The Impact on Relationships

The empathy deficit in narcissistic personality styles can have a profound impact on relationships. It can leave partners, family members, and friends feeling emotionally neglected, invalidated, and unimportant. The lack of empathy can create a dynamic where the needs and feelings of the narcissist take precedence, leading to a one-sided and unbalanced relationship.

Furthermore, the lack of emotional connection can make it challenging for individuals in relationships with narcissists to feel understood and supported. They may struggle to communicate their needs and emotions effectively, as the narcissist may dismiss or minimize their experiences. This can lead to feelings of frustration, isolation, and a sense of being unheard.

4.4.8 Navigating the Empathy Deficit

Navigating the empathy deficit in relationships with narcissistic individuals can be challenging, but it is essential to prioritize self-care and establish healthy boundaries. Recognizing that the lack of empathy is a core feature of narcissism can help individuals understand that it is not a reflection of their worth or value.

It is crucial to seek support from trusted friends, family, or professionals who can provide validation and understanding. Engaging in self-care activities, such as therapy, mindfulness practices, and self-reflection, can also help individuals cope with the emotional toll of being in a relationship with a narcissist.

Additionally, setting clear boundaries and communicating assertively can help protect one's emotional well-being. It is important to establish limits on what is acceptable behavior and to communicate these boundaries clearly and consistently. This can help individuals maintain their sense of self and protect themselves from emotional manipulation.

4.4.9 Building Empathy in Relationships

While it may be challenging to foster empathy in individuals with narcissistic personality styles, it is not impossible. However, it requires a willingness on the part of the narcissist to acknowledge and address their narcissistic tendencies. Therapy and self-reflection can be valuable tools in helping individuals with narcissistic traits develop a greater capacity for empathy and emotional connection.

In conclusion, the empathy deficit is a significant aspect of narcissistic personality styles. Understanding the lack of emotional connection and the self-centered focus can help individuals navigate relationships with narcissists more effectively. Prioritizing self-care, setting boundaries, and seeking support are essential for maintaining emotional well-being in relationships with narcissistic individuals.

5

Chapter 5

Healing and Recovery

5.1 Recognizing and Overcoming Self-Blame

When it comes to dealing with narcissistic personality styles, one of the most challenging aspects for survivors is recognizing and overcoming self-blame. Narcissists are skilled manipulators who often make their victims question their own worth and sanity. As a result, it is common for individuals who have been in relationships with narcissists to blame themselves for the abuse they endured. In this section, we will explore the reasons behind self-blame and provide strategies for overcoming it.

Understanding the Dynamics of Narcissistic Relationships

Before delving into self-blame, it is crucial to understand the dynamics of narcissistic relationships. Narcissists possess an inflated sense of self-importance and a deep need for admiration. They lack empathy and exploit others for their own gain. In romantic relationships, narcissists often engage in a cycle of idealization, devaluation, and discard. They shower their partners with love and attention in the beginning, only to gradually devalue and manipulate them over time.

The Role of Self-Blame in Narcissistic Relationships

Self-blame is a common response to narcissistic abuse. Victims often question their own actions and choices, believing that they must have done something to provoke the narcissist's behavior. This self-blame can be reinforced by the narcissist, who may gaslight their partner into believing that they are the problem. The narcissist's manipulation and charm can make it difficult for victims to see the abuse for what it truly is.

Overcoming Self-Blame

Recognizing and overcoming self-blame is an essential step towards healing and recovery. Here are some strategies to help you on this journey:

1. Educate Yourself

Understanding narcissistic personality styles and the tactics they employ is crucial in overcoming self-blame. By learning about the disorder, you can gain insight into the manipulative techniques used by narcissists. This knowledge will help you realize that the abuse was not your fault and that you were targeted because of the narcissist's own insecurities.

2. Seek Support

Building a support network is vital in overcoming self-blame. Reach out to trusted friends, family members, or support groups who can provide validation and understanding. Sharing your experiences with others who have been through similar situations can help you realize that you are not alone and that the blame lies with the narcissist, not with yourself.

3. Practice Self-Compassion

Be kind to yourself and practice self-compassion. Understand that you were manipulated and deceived by a skilled manipulator. Treat yourself with the same empathy and understanding that you would offer to a friend in a similar situation. Remind yourself that you deserve love, respect, and happiness.

4. Challenge Negative Self-Talk

Narcissists often instill negative beliefs in their victims, leading to a destructive internal dialogue. Challenge these negative thoughts by replacing them with positive affirmations. Remind yourself of your strengths, accomplishments, and the qualities that make you unique. Surround yourself with positive influences that reinforce your self-worth.

5. Seek Professional Help

If self-blame persists and affects your daily life, seeking professional help from a therapist or counselor can be beneficial. A mental health professional can provide guidance and support as you navigate the healing process. They can help you reframe your experiences, develop coping strategies, and rebuild your self-esteem.

Moving Towards Self-Acceptance and Healing

Overcoming self-blame is a gradual process that requires patience and self-reflection. It is important to remember that you are not to blame for the narcissist's actions. By recognizing the tactics used by narcissists, seeking support, practicing self-compassion, challenging negative self-talk, and seeking professional help if needed, you can begin to heal and move towards self-acceptance.

Remember, you are not alone in your experiences. Many individuals have been in relationships with narcissists and have faced similar challenges. By sharing your story, seeking support, and educating others about narcissistic personality styles, you can help break the cycle of abuse and empower others to recognize and overcome self-blame.

5.2 Support Systems: Finding Help and Building a Support Network

Building a support network is crucial for survivors of narcissistic abuse. In this section, we will explore the importance of support systems and provide guidance on finding help and building a network of support.

The Importance of Support

Recovering from narcissistic abuse can be a long and challenging journey. Having a support system in place can provide validation, understanding, and encouragement. Supportive individuals can help you navigate the healing process, offer a listening ear, and provide a safe space for you to share your experiences.

Finding Help

Finding professional help is an essential step in healing from narcissistic abuse. Therapists and counselors who specialize in trauma and abuse can provide guidance, validation, and tools to help you overcome the effects of the abuse. They can help you process your emotions, develop coping strategies, and rebuild your self-esteem.

When seeking professional help, it is important to find a therapist or counselor who understands narcissistic personality styles and has experience working with survivors of narcissistic abuse. They should create a safe and non-judgmental environment where you can explore your experiences and emotions.

Building a Support Network

In addition to professional help, building a support network of friends, family, and fellow survivors is crucial. Here are some steps to help you build a strong support network:

1. Identify Trusted Individuals

Identify individuals in your life who are supportive, understanding, and empathetic. These can be friends, family members, or even support groups. Look for people who validate your experiences and provide a safe space for you to share your thoughts and emotions.

2. Communicate Your Needs

Once you have identified supportive individuals, communicate your needs to them. Let them know how they can best support you, whether it's by simply listening, offering advice, or providing a distraction when needed. Be open and honest about your experiences and emotions, as this will help them better understand your journey.

3. Join Support Groups

Consider joining support groups or online communities specifically for survivors of narcissistic abuse. These groups provide a platform to connect with others who have had similar experiences. Sharing your story and hearing from others can be incredibly validating and empowering. It can also provide you with a sense of belonging and support.

4. Set Boundaries

While building a support network is important, it is equally important to set boundaries. Not everyone in your life may be capable of providing the support you need, and that's okay. It's essential to prioritize your well-being and surround yourself with individuals who uplift and validate you. Set boundaries with those who may not understand or support your healing journey.

5. Seek Online Resources

In addition to in-person support, there are numerous online resources available for survivors of narcissistic abuse. Websites, forums, and blogs dedicated to narcissistic abuse can provide valuable information, validation, and support. Engaging with these resources can help you feel less alone and provide additional tools for healing.

The Power of Support

Building a support network is a powerful tool in the healing process. Surrounding yourself with understanding and empathetic individuals can help you overcome self-blame, validate your experiences, and provide the encouragement needed to move forward. Remember, you are not alone, and there are people who genuinely care and want to support you on your journey to healing and recovery.

5.2 Support Systems

Support systems play a crucial role in helping individuals understand and navigate the complexities of narcissistic personality styles. Whether you are currently in a relationship with a narcissist, have recently ended one, or are seeking to avoid getting involved with a narcissist in the future, having a strong support network can make a significant difference in your healing and recovery process. In this section, we will explore the importance of support systems, how to find help, and how to build a support network that can aid you in understanding and surviving narcissistic personality styles.

5.2.1 The Importance of Support Systems

Dealing with narcissistic personality styles can be emotionally draining and challenging. It is essential to recognize that you are not alone in this experience. Many individuals have encountered narcissists in their lives and have successfully navigated through the difficulties associated with these relationships. Having a support system can provide you with the validation, empathy, and guidance needed to heal and move forward.

Support systems can come in various forms, including friends, family, therapists, support groups, and online communities. These individuals and resources can offer a safe space for you to share your experiences, gain insights, and receive emotional support. They can also provide you with a different perspective, helping you see the situation more clearly and empowering you to make informed decisions.

5.2.2 Finding Help

When dealing with narcissistic personality styles, seeking professional help is often beneficial. Therapists who specialize in narcissistic abuse can provide you with the necessary tools and strategies to heal from the emotional trauma inflicted by narcissists. They can guide you through the process of rebuilding your self-esteem, setting healthy boundaries, and developing healthier relationship patterns.

Additionally, support groups specifically tailored for individuals who have experienced narcissistic abuse can be invaluable. These groups offer a sense of community and understanding, allowing you to connect with others who have gone through similar experiences. Sharing your stories and listening to others can provide validation and help you realize that you are not alone.

Online resources, such as websites, forums, and social media groups, can also be valuable sources of support. These platforms allow you to connect with individuals who have firsthand experience with narcissistic personality styles. Engaging in discussions, reading articles, and sharing your own insights can contribute to your healing journey.

5.2.3 Building a Support Network

In addition to seeking professional help and utilizing online resources, building a support network of trusted individuals is crucial. Here are some steps to help you establish a strong support system:

1. Identify trustworthy individuals: Look for friends, family members, or colleagues who have shown empathy, understanding, and a willingness to support you. These individuals should be non-judgmental and able to provide a safe space for you to express your feelings.
2. Communicate your needs: Clearly communicate your experiences,

emotions, and needs to your support network. Let them know how they can best support you, whether it's through active listening, offering advice, or simply being there for you.

3. Set boundaries: It is essential to establish boundaries with your support network. Clearly communicate what you are comfortable discussing and what topics may be triggering for you. This will help ensure that your interactions remain supportive and respectful.

4. Seek professional guidance: Encourage your support network to educate themselves about narcissistic personality styles and the impact they can have on relationships. This will enable them to provide more informed support and guidance.

5. Attend support groups: Consider joining local support groups or online communities where you can connect with others who have experienced narcissistic abuse. These groups can provide a sense of belonging and understanding that is crucial for healing.

Remember, building a support network takes time and effort. Be patient with yourself and those around you as you navigate through this process. Surrounding yourself with individuals who genuinely care about your well-being can make a significant difference in your healing journey.

Conclusion

Support systems are an essential component of understanding and surviving narcissistic personality styles. They provide validation, empathy, and guidance, helping individuals heal from the emotional trauma inflicted by narcissists. By seeking professional help, utilizing online resources, and building a support network, you can empower yourself to overcome the challenges associated with narcissistic relationships. Remember, you are not alone, and with the right support, you can heal, rebuild your self-esteem, and move forward towards a healthier and more fulfilling life.

5.3 Rebuilding Self-Esteem and Self-Worth

Recovering from a relationship with a narcissistic personality style can be an arduous journey, but it is essential to rebuild your self-esteem and self-worth. The emotional and psychological toll of being involved with a narcissist can leave you feeling depleted, unworthy, and questioning your own value. However, it is important to remember that you are not to blame for the narcissist's behavior. Many individuals have found themselves entangled in relationships with narcissists, and it is crucial to recognize that you are not alone in this experience.

Understanding the Impact on Self-Esteem

One of the most significant effects of being in a relationship with a narcissist is the erosion of self-esteem. Narcissists often employ manipulative tactics such as gaslighting, belittling, and demeaning their partners to maintain control and power. Over time, these tactics can chip away at your self-confidence and self-worth, leaving you feeling inadequate and unworthy of love and respect.

It is important to recognize that the narcissist's behavior is a reflection of their own insecurities and not a reflection of your worth as an individual. Rebuilding your self-esteem starts with understanding that you are deserving of love, respect, and happiness. Surround yourself with supportive and empathetic individuals who can help you regain your sense of self-worth.

Cultivating Self-Compassion

Rebuilding self-esteem and self-worth after a relationship with a narcissist requires practicing self-compassion. It is crucial to be kind and understanding towards yourself, acknowledging that you have been through a challenging experience. Allow yourself to grieve the loss of the relationship and the emotional turmoil it caused.

Practice self-care by engaging in activities that bring you joy and fulfillment.

Take time to nurture your physical, emotional, and mental well-being. Engage in activities that promote self-reflection and personal growth, such as journaling, meditation, or therapy. These practices can help you develop a deeper understanding of yourself and rebuild your self-esteem from within.

Challenging Negative Self-Talk

During and after a relationship with a narcissist, it is common to internalize their negative messages and develop a pattern of negative self-talk. This negative self-talk can further damage your self-esteem and hinder your ability to rebuild your sense of self-worth. It is crucial to challenge these negative thoughts and replace them with positive and affirming beliefs about yourself.

Start by identifying the negative thoughts that arise and question their validity. Ask yourself if there is evidence to support these thoughts or if they are merely remnants of the narcissist's manipulation. Replace these negative thoughts with positive affirmations and reminders of your strengths and worthiness. Surround yourself with positive influences and seek support from friends, family, or support groups who can reinforce your positive self-perception.

Setting Boundaries and Prioritizing Self-Care

Rebuilding self-esteem and self-worth also involves setting healthy boundaries and prioritizing self-care. Establish clear boundaries with the narcissist, whether it is through limited contact or complete separation. Understand that you have the right to protect yourself from further emotional harm and prioritize your well-being.

Practice assertiveness and self-advocacy by communicating your needs and desires effectively. Surround yourself with individuals who respect and support your boundaries. Engage in activities that promote self-care, such as exercise, hobbies, and spending time with loved ones. Prioritize your emotional well-being and make self-care a non-negotiable part of your daily routine.

Seeking Professional Help

Rebuilding self-esteem and self-worth after a relationship with a narcissist can be a complex and challenging process. It is essential to seek professional help if you find yourself struggling to heal and regain your sense of self. Therapists specializing in trauma and narcissistic abuse can provide valuable guidance and support as you navigate the healing process.

Therapy can help you process the emotional wounds inflicted by the narcissist, develop healthy coping mechanisms, and rebuild your self-esteem. A therapist can also assist you in identifying and addressing any underlying issues that may have contributed to your vulnerability to narcissistic abuse.

Remember, healing takes time, and everyone's journey is unique. Be patient and compassionate with yourself as you rebuild your self-esteem and self-worth. Surround yourself with a supportive network of individuals who uplift and validate your experiences. With time, self-reflection, and professional guidance, you can emerge from the shadows of narcissistic abuse and reclaim your sense of self-worth and happiness.

5.4 Moving Forward

Moving forward after experiencing a relationship with a narcissistic personality can be a challenging and transformative journey. It is essential to prioritize your healing and well-being, and part of that process involves setting healthy boundaries and learning to trust again. In this section, we will explore strategies for moving forward, rebuilding your life, and creating healthier relationships.

5.4.1 Setting Healthy Boundaries

One of the most crucial steps in moving forward after a relationship with a narcissist is setting healthy boundaries. Narcissists often disregard boundaries and manipulate others to meet their own needs. As a survivor, it is essential to establish clear boundaries to protect yourself from further harm.

Here are some strategies to help you set and maintain healthy boundaries:

1. **Identify your needs and values:** Take the time to reflect on your needs and values. What are your non-negotiables in a relationship? Understanding your own boundaries will help you communicate them effectively to others.

2. **Communicate assertively:** Practice assertive communication to express your boundaries clearly and confidently. Use "I" statements to express your needs and expectations without blaming or attacking the other person.

3. **Recognize red flags:** Be vigilant for red flags in new relationships. Look out for signs of manipulation, lack of empathy, and entitlement. Trust your instincts and be willing to walk away if you sense any warning signs.

4. **Practice self-care:** Prioritize self-care and self-love. Engage in activities that bring you joy, relaxation, and fulfillment. Taking care of yourself will help you maintain healthy boundaries and attract healthier relationships.

5. **Seek support:** Surround yourself with a supportive network of friends, family, or a therapist who can provide guidance and encouragement as you navigate setting boundaries. They can offer valuable insights and help you stay accountable.

5.4.2 Rebuilding Trust

After experiencing a relationship with a narcissist, it is natural to feel a loss of trust in others. Rebuilding trust is a gradual process that requires self-reflection, healing, and learning from past experiences. Here are some steps to help you rebuild trust:

1. **Self-reflection:** Take the time to reflect on your past relationship and identify patterns or behaviors that contributed to the dynamic with the narcissist. This self-reflection will help you gain insight into your own

vulnerabilities and make healthier choices moving forward.

2. **Seek professional help:** Consider seeking therapy or counseling to work through the emotional wounds caused by the narcissistic relationship. A trained professional can guide you through the healing process and help you rebuild trust in yourself and others.

3. **Start small:** Begin by trusting yourself. Listen to your intuition and honor your feelings and needs. As you regain trust in your own judgment, you will become more confident in trusting others.

4. **Take it slow:** When entering new relationships, take your time to get to know the person and build trust gradually. Allow the relationship to develop naturally and pay attention to how the other person respects your boundaries and treats you.

5. **Practice forgiveness:** Forgiving the narcissist may not be necessary or even possible, but forgiving yourself is crucial. Release any self-blame or guilt you may be carrying and focus on your own growth and healing.

5.4.3 Trusting Again

Trusting again after experiencing a relationship with a narcissist can be a daunting task. However, it is important to remember that not everyone possesses narcissistic traits. Here are some tips to help you navigate trust in future relationships:

1. **Take your time:** Allow trust to develop naturally. Rushing into a new relationship may make it difficult to discern whether the person is genuinely trustworthy or not. Take the time to observe their actions and consistency over an extended period.

2. **Observe their behavior:** Pay attention to how the person treats others, including friends, family, and strangers. Look for signs of empathy, respect, and genuine care for others. A person's behavior towards others can be a good indicator of their character.

3. **Communicate openly:** Share your concerns and fears about trust with your partner. Open and honest communication is essential for building

trust. A trustworthy partner will be understanding and supportive of your journey to rebuild trust.

4. **Seek professional guidance:** If you find it challenging to trust again, consider seeking therapy or counseling. A therapist can help you work through any lingering fears or anxieties and provide guidance on building trust in future relationships.

Remember, healing takes time, and it is okay to be cautious when entering new relationships. Trust is earned, and by setting healthy boundaries, practicing self-care, and seeking support, you can gradually rebuild trust and create healthier connections.

Conclusion

Moving forward after a relationship with a narcissistic personality style is a process of self-discovery, healing, and growth. It is important to remember that you are not alone in this journey. Many people have experienced similar relationships and have successfully rebuilt their lives.

By setting healthy boundaries, rebuilding trust, and surrounding yourself with a supportive network, you can create a life of authenticity and fulfillment. Remember to prioritize self-care, practice self-compassion, and embrace the journey of healing and resilience.

In the next chapter, we will explore strategies for preventing and protecting yourself from narcissistic relationships. We will discuss early warning signs, developing healthy relationship patterns, and the importance of self-care and self-love.

6

Chapter 6

Prevention and Self-Protection

6.1 Identifying Early Warning Signs

When it comes to narcissistic personality styles, prevention and self-protection are crucial. By identifying the early warning signs, you can avoid getting involved in toxic relationships with narcissists. This section will provide you with insights into recognizing these warning signs and protecting yourself from potential harm.

6.1.1 Understanding Narcissistic Personality Styles

Before delving into the early warning signs, it's important to have a clear understanding of narcissistic personality styles. Narcissism exists on a spectrum, with both covert and overt traits. Covert narcissists tend to be more subtle in their behaviors, often appearing shy or introverted. They may manipulate others through passive-aggressive tactics, emotional manipulation, and playing the victim. Overt narcissists, on the other hand, display more obvious traits such as grandiosity, arrogance, and a constant need for attention and admiration.

It's important to note that narcissism can vary in severity and presentation. Some individuals may exhibit only a few narcissistic traits, while others may have a full-blown narcissistic personality disorder. Understanding these variations can help you recognize the signs early on and protect yourself from potential harm.

6.1.2 Red Flags in Romantic Relationships

When it comes to dating, it's crucial to be aware of the red flags that may indicate a potential narcissistic partner. While not all individuals who display these traits are narcissists, these signs can serve as a warning to proceed with caution. Some common red flags include:

1. **Excessive self-focus:** Narcissists often prioritize their own needs and desires above others. They may constantly talk about themselves, show little interest in your life, and dismiss your feelings and opinions.
2. **Lack of empathy:** Narcissists struggle to empathize with others and may disregard or invalidate your emotions. They may also lack the ability to take responsibility for their actions and apologize sincerely.
3. **Sense of entitlement:** Narcissists often believe they are special and deserving of special treatment. They may expect you to cater to their every need and become angry or resentful when their expectations are not met.
4. **Manipulative behavior:** Narcissists are skilled manipulators and may use tactics such as gaslighting, guilt-tripping, and love bombing to control and manipulate their partners.
5. **Constant need for validation:** Narcissists crave constant attention, admiration, and validation. They may seek validation from multiple sources, including flirting with others or engaging in extramarital affairs.
6. **Lack of boundaries:** Narcissists often have difficulty respecting boundaries and may invade your personal space, both physically and emotionally. They may also try to isolate you from friends and family,

making you dependent on them.

7. **Intense charm followed by devaluation:** Narcissists often employ a cycle of idealization and devaluation in their relationships. They may shower you with love and affection in the beginning, only to devalue and criticize you later on.

It's important to trust your instincts and take these red flags seriously. If you notice several of these warning signs in a potential partner, it may be wise to reconsider the relationship and prioritize your own well-being.

6.1.3 Developing Healthy Relationship Patterns

To avoid getting involved in narcissistic relationships, it's essential to develop healthy relationship patterns. This involves understanding your own needs, setting boundaries, and being assertive in your communication. Here are some tips to help you establish healthy relationship patterns:

1. **Know your worth:** Recognize your own value and worthiness of love and respect. Build your self-esteem and self-confidence, so you are less likely to tolerate mistreatment or settle for less than you deserve.
2. **Set clear boundaries:** Establish clear boundaries and communicate them openly and assertively. Be firm in enforcing your boundaries and do not compromise on your values and needs.
3. **Take it slow:** Avoid rushing into relationships and take the time to get to know someone before becoming emotionally invested. This allows you to observe their behavior and identify any potential red flags.
4. **Seek support:** Surround yourself with a strong support network of friends and family who can provide guidance and support. They can offer an outside perspective and help you recognize any warning signs you may have missed.
5. **Listen to your intuition:** Trust your gut instincts. If something feels off or doesn't align with your values, take a step back and reassess the situation. Your intuition can often guide you towards healthier choices.

6. **Educate yourself:** Learn more about narcissistic personality styles and the tactics they employ. By educating yourself, you become better equipped to identify and avoid potential narcissistic partners.

Remember, developing healthy relationship patterns takes time and practice. Be patient with yourself and trust that you have the power to create fulfilling and healthy connections.

6.1.4 Assertiveness and Self-Advocacy: Protecting Yourself

Assertiveness and self-advocacy are essential skills when it comes to protecting yourself from narcissistic individuals. By asserting your needs and boundaries, you establish a strong foundation for healthy relationships. Here are some strategies to help you become more assertive:

1. **Practice self-awareness:** Understand your own needs, values, and boundaries. This self-awareness will enable you to clearly communicate your expectations to others.
2. **Use "I" statements:** When expressing your needs or concerns, use "I" statements to avoid sounding accusatory. For example, say "I feel hurt when you dismiss my opinions" instead of "You always ignore me."
3. **Be direct and specific:** Clearly communicate your boundaries and expectations. Avoid vague statements and be specific about what you will and will not tolerate in a relationship.
4. **Stay calm and composed:** Maintain a calm and composed demeanor when asserting yourself. This will help you convey your message effectively and avoid escalating conflicts.
5. **Practice active listening:** Actively listen to the other person's perspective and validate their feelings. This promotes open communication and can help build healthier relationships.
6. **Seek professional help if needed:** If you struggle with assertiveness, consider seeking the guidance of a therapist or counselor. They can provide you with tools and techniques to improve your assertiveness

skills.

Remember, being assertive does not mean being aggressive or disrespectful. It is about expressing your needs and boundaries in a clear and respectful manner.

6.1.5 Self-Care and Self-Love: Nurturing Your Emotional Well-being

In the journey of avoiding narcissistic relationships, self-care and self-love play a vital role. Prioritizing your emotional well-being is essential for building resilience and protecting yourself from toxic dynamics. Here are some self-care practices to incorporate into your life:

1. **Set aside "me" time:** Dedicate regular time to engage in activities that bring you joy and relaxation. This could include hobbies, self-reflection, or simply taking a break from daily stressors.
2. **Practice self-compassion:** Be kind and compassionate towards yourself. Treat yourself with the same love and understanding you would offer a dear friend.
3. **Establish healthy boundaries:** Set boundaries not only with others but also with yourself. Learn to say no to activities or commitments that drain your energy or compromise your well-being.
4. **Nurture your physical health:** Engage in regular exercise, eat a balanced diet, and prioritize sufficient sleep. Taking care of your physical health can positively impact your emotional well-being.
5. **Seek support:** Reach out to trusted friends, family, or support groups who can provide a safe space for you to share your experiences and emotions. Surrounding yourself with a supportive network can be immensely healing.
6. **Practice mindfulness:** Cultivate mindfulness through meditation, deep breathing exercises, or other mindfulness techniques. This helps you stay present, manage stress, and cultivate self-awareness.

Remember, self-care is not selfish; it is a necessary act of self-preservation. By prioritizing your emotional well-being, you empower yourself to make healthier choices and build fulfilling relationships.

In the next section, we will explore the importance of developing healthy relationship patterns and delve into the topic of assertiveness and self-advocacy in more detail.

6.2 Developing Healthy Relationship Patterns

Developing healthy relationship patterns is crucial for individuals who have experienced or are at risk of being involved with narcissistic personality styles. By understanding the traits and dynamics of narcissistic relationships, individuals can learn to recognize and avoid potential partners who exhibit these traits. Additionally, developing healthy relationship patterns involves setting boundaries, practicing assertiveness, and prioritizing self-care. In this section, we will explore strategies and techniques to help individuals develop healthy relationship patterns and protect themselves from narcissistic personality styles.

6.2.1 Recognizing and Avoiding Narcissistic Relationships

One of the most effective ways to protect oneself from narcissistic relationships is to develop the ability to recognize early warning signs. By being aware of these signs, individuals can avoid getting involved with potential partners who exhibit narcissistic traits. Some red flags to look out for when dating include:

1. **Excessive self-focus**: Narcissists often prioritize their own needs and desires above others. They may constantly talk about themselves, show little interest in your life, and dismiss your feelings and opinions.
2. **Lack of empathy**: Narcissists struggle to empathize with others and often disregard or invalidate their emotions. They may appear indifferent or dismissive when you express your feelings or needs.

3. **Grandiose sense of self-importance**: Narcissists often have an inflated sense of self-worth and believe they are superior to others. They may constantly seek admiration and attention, and expect special treatment.

4. **Manipulative behavior**: Narcissists are skilled manipulators who use tactics such as gaslighting, guilt-tripping, and emotional blackmail to control and dominate their partners. They may also engage in love-bombing, showering you with excessive affection and attention in the early stages of the relationship.

5. **Lack of accountability**: Narcissists rarely take responsibility for their actions and tend to blame others for their mistakes or shortcomings. They may exhibit a pattern of shifting blame and avoiding accountability.

6. **Boundary violations**: Narcissists often disregard personal boundaries and may invade your privacy, make decisions without consulting you, or pressure you into doing things you're uncomfortable with.

By being mindful of these red flags, individuals can make informed decisions about their relationships and avoid getting entangled with narcissistic partners. It's important to remember that not all individuals who exhibit these traits are narcissists, but recognizing these warning signs can help individuals protect themselves from potentially harmful relationships.

6.2.2 Setting Boundaries and Practicing Assertiveness

Developing healthy relationship patterns involves setting and maintaining clear boundaries. Narcissists often have difficulty respecting boundaries, so it's essential to establish and communicate your limits early on in the relationship. Here are some strategies for setting boundaries with narcissistic individuals:

1. **Identify your needs and values**: Take the time to reflect on your own needs, values, and boundaries. This self-awareness will help you

communicate your boundaries effectively.

2. **Communicate assertively**: Clearly and confidently express your boundaries to your partner. Use "I" statements to express how their behavior affects you and what you need from the relationship.

3. **Be consistent**: Consistently reinforce your boundaries by following through with consequences if they are violated. This will help establish a sense of accountability and respect in the relationship.

4. **Seek support**: Reach out to trusted friends, family, or a therapist for support and guidance in setting and maintaining boundaries. They can provide valuable insights and help you stay accountable.

6.2.3 Prioritizing Self-Care and Emotional Well-being

In order to develop healthy relationship patterns, it is crucial to prioritize self-care and emotional well-being. Here are some strategies to nurture your emotional well-being:

1. **Practice self-compassion**: Be kind and understanding towards yourself. Recognize that you are not to blame for the actions of a narcissistic partner and that healing takes time.

2. **Engage in self-care activities**: Take time for activities that bring you joy and relaxation. This can include hobbies, exercise, spending time in nature, or practicing mindfulness and meditation.

3. **Build a support network**: Surround yourself with supportive and understanding individuals who can provide emotional support and validation. Joining support groups or seeking therapy can also be beneficial in the healing process.

4. **Set realistic expectations**: Understand that healing from a narcissistic relationship takes time and effort. Be patient with yourself and allow yourself to grieve the loss of the relationship.

By prioritizing self-care and emotional well-being, individuals can rebuild their sense of self-worth and develop healthier relationship patterns. It is important to remember that healing is a journey, and with time and support, individuals can move forward and thrive after narcissistic abuse.

Conclusion

Developing healthy relationship patterns is essential for individuals who have experienced or are at risk of being involved with narcissistic personality styles. By recognizing early warning signs, setting boundaries, and prioritizing self-care, individuals can protect themselves from potentially harmful relationships. It is important to remember that healing and recovery take time, and seeking support from trusted individuals can greatly aid in the process. By developing healthy relationship patterns, individuals can create fulfilling and authentic connections, free from the detrimental effects of narcissistic personality styles.

6.3 Assertiveness and Self-Advocacy

Assertiveness and self-advocacy are crucial skills for protecting yourself from the harmful effects of narcissistic personality styles. When dealing with individuals who exhibit narcissistic traits, it is essential to establish and maintain healthy boundaries, communicate your needs effectively, and assert your rights. This section will provide you with practical strategies and techniques to develop assertiveness and self-advocacy skills, empowering you to protect yourself from narcissistic abuse.

6.3.1 Understanding Assertiveness

Assertiveness is the ability to express your thoughts, feelings, and needs in a direct, honest, and respectful manner. It involves standing up for yourself while considering the rights and feelings of others. Assertive communication allows you to express your boundaries, assert your needs, and address conflicts effectively. When dealing with narcissistic individuals, assertiveness is crucial to protect your emotional well-being and maintain healthy relationships.

6.3.2 Developing Assertiveness Skills

Developing assertiveness skills can be challenging, especially if you have experienced narcissistic abuse. However, with practice and self-reflection, you can cultivate assertiveness and advocate for yourself. Here are some strategies to help you develop assertiveness skills:

1. **Self-awareness:** Start by becoming aware of your thoughts, feelings, and needs. Understand your boundaries and what you are comfortable with in different situations. This self-awareness will provide a foundation for assertive communication.

2. **Practice active listening:** Effective communication involves not only expressing yourself but also actively listening to others. Practice active listening by giving your full attention, maintaining eye contact, and validating the speaker's feelings. This will help build rapport and understanding in your interactions.

3. **Use "I" statements:** When expressing your needs or concerns, use "I" statements to take ownership of your feelings and experiences. For example, instead of saying, "You always make me feel inadequate," say, "I feel inadequate when you criticize me." This approach avoids blaming the other person and focuses on your emotions.

4. **Set clear boundaries:** Establishing and communicating your boundaries is essential when dealing with narcissistic individuals. Clearly define what is acceptable and unacceptable behavior for you. Communicate these boundaries assertively and consistently, reinforcing them when necessary.

5. **Practice saying no:** Saying no is an important aspect of assertiveness. Practice saying no to requests or demands that do not align with your values or priorities. Remember, it is okay to prioritize your well-being and say no when necessary.

6. **Use assertive body language:** Non-verbal cues play a significant role

in communication. Maintain good posture, make eye contact, and use confident body language when expressing yourself. This will enhance the impact of your assertive communication.

7. **Practice assertive responses:** Role-play different scenarios to practice assertive responses. This can help you build confidence and develop effective communication strategies when dealing with narcissistic individuals.

6.3.3 Self-Advocacy: Protecting Yourself

Self-advocacy goes beyond assertiveness and involves actively advocating for your rights, needs, and well-being. When dealing with narcissistic individuals, self-advocacy is crucial to protect yourself from manipulation and abuse. Here are some strategies to help you become a strong self-advocate:

1. **Educate yourself:** Learn about narcissistic personality styles and the tactics they employ. Understanding their behaviors and manipulation techniques will empower you to recognize and respond effectively to their actions.

2. **Build a support network:** Surround yourself with trusted friends, family, or support groups who understand and validate your experiences. Having a support network can provide emotional support, guidance, and validation during challenging times.

3. **Document incidents:** Keep a record of incidents where you have experienced narcissistic abuse. Documenting specific instances of manipulation, gaslighting, or emotional abuse can help you validate your experiences and provide evidence if needed.

4. **Seek professional help:** Consider seeking therapy or counseling to help you heal from the effects of narcissistic abuse. A mental health professional can provide guidance, support, and strategies to rebuild your self-esteem and navigate challenging relationships.

5. **Practice self-care:** Prioritize self-care activities that nurture your

emotional well-being. Engage in activities that bring you joy, practice mindfulness, and take care of your physical health. Self-care is essential for rebuilding your sense of self-worth and resilience.

6. **Set and enforce boundaries:** Clearly define your boundaries and communicate them assertively. Be prepared to enforce consequences if your boundaries are violated. Narcissistic individuals often test boundaries, and it is crucial to stand firm in protecting your well-being.

7. **Limit contact or cut ties:** In some cases, limiting or cutting off contact with narcissistic individuals may be necessary for your emotional well-being. Assess the relationship and consider whether it is healthy and beneficial for you. Remember, prioritizing your safety and well-being is not selfish; it is an act of self-preservation.

Conclusion

Developing assertiveness and self-advocacy skills is essential for protecting yourself from the harmful effects of narcissistic personality styles. By cultivating these skills, you can establish healthy boundaries, communicate effectively, and advocate for your rights and well-being. Remember, you have the power to protect yourself and create a life free from narcissistic abuse.

6.4 Self-Care and Self-Love

When dealing with the aftermath of a relationship with a narcissistic individual, it is crucial to prioritize self-care and self-love. The emotional toll of being involved with a narcissist can be significant, and it is essential to take the time to heal and rebuild your emotional well-being. In this chapter, we will explore various strategies and techniques to nurture your emotional well-being and regain your sense of self.

6.4.1 Prioritizing Your Needs

One of the most important aspects of self-care is prioritizing your needs. After being in a relationship with a narcissist, it is common to have neglected your own needs and desires. Take the time to identify what brings you joy and fulfillment, and make a conscious effort to incorporate these activities into your daily life. Whether it's engaging in hobbies, spending time with loved ones, or practicing self-reflection, prioritize activities that nourish your soul and bring you happiness.

6.4.2 Setting Boundaries

Setting healthy boundaries is crucial when it comes to protecting yourself from further harm. Narcissists often have a disregard for boundaries and may try to manipulate or exploit you. It is essential to establish clear boundaries and communicate them assertively. Remember that it is okay to say no and prioritize your well-being. Surround yourself with people who respect your boundaries and support your journey towards healing.

6.4.3 Practicing Self-Compassion

After experiencing the emotional manipulation and abuse of a narcissistic relationship, it is common to blame yourself or question your worth. It is important to remember that you are not to blame for the narcissist's behavior. Practice self-compassion by treating yourself with kindness and understanding. Remind yourself that you deserve love, respect, and happiness. Engage in positive self-talk and challenge any negative beliefs that the narcissist may have instilled in you.

6.4.4 Seeking Support

Building a support network is crucial in the healing process. Reach out to trusted friends, family members, or support groups who can provide a safe space for you to share your experiences and emotions. Surrounding yourself with individuals who understand and validate your feelings can be incredibly empowering. Additionally, consider seeking professional help from therapists or counselors who specialize in narcissistic abuse. They can provide guidance and support as you navigate the healing process.

6.4.5 Engaging in Self-Reflection

Self-reflection is a powerful tool for personal growth and healing. Take the time to reflect on your past relationship and identify patterns or red flags that you may have missed. This self-awareness will help you avoid similar situations in the future. Journaling can be a helpful practice to explore your emotions, thoughts, and experiences. By gaining a deeper understanding of yourself and your needs, you can make more informed choices in future relationships.

6.4.6 Practicing Mindfulness

Mindfulness is a practice that involves being fully present in the moment and non-judgmentally observing your thoughts and emotions. Engaging in mindfulness exercises, such as meditation or deep breathing, can help reduce stress and anxiety. It allows you to cultivate inner strength and resilience, enabling you to navigate challenging situations with greater ease. By practicing mindfulness, you can develop a stronger connection with yourself and your emotions.

6.4.7 Nurturing Your Physical Health

Taking care of your physical health is an essential aspect of self-care. Engage in regular exercise, eat a balanced diet, and prioritize getting enough sleep. Physical activity releases endorphins, which can boost your mood and overall well-being. Nourishing your body with nutritious food and adequate rest will provide you with the energy and vitality needed to heal and thrive.

6.4.8 Embracing Growth and Resilience

Remember that healing from the effects of a narcissistic relationship is a journey. Embrace the process of growth and resilience as you rebuild your life. Celebrate your progress, no matter how small, and acknowledge the strength and courage it takes to move forward. Surround yourself with positive influences and engage in activities that inspire and uplift you. By focusing on personal growth and embracing resilience, you can create a life filled with authenticity, fulfillment, and healthy relationships.

In conclusion, self-care and self-love are essential components of healing and recovering from a relationship with a narcissistic individual. Prioritizing your needs, setting boundaries, practicing self-compassion, seeking support, engaging in self-reflection, practicing mindfulness, nurturing your physical health, and embracing growth and resilience are all crucial steps in the journey towards healing and thriving. Remember that you are not alone, and with time and self-care, you can rebuild your life and create healthy, fulfilling relationships.

7

Chapter 7

Understanding Narcissism in Males

7.1 Societal Expectations and Male Narcissism

Societal expectations play a significant role in shaping the development and manifestation of narcissistic personality styles in males. From a young age, boys are often socialized to be assertive, confident, and dominant. These traits, when taken to an extreme, can contribute to the development of narcissistic tendencies. Society often rewards and reinforces behaviors associated with narcissism, such as self-promotion, competitiveness, and the pursuit of power and success. As a result, many men may feel pressured to adopt narcissistic traits in order to meet societal expectations of masculinity.

7.1.1 The Influence of Societal Stereotypes

Societal stereotypes surrounding masculinity can contribute to the development and perpetuation of male narcissism. Traditional gender roles often emphasize the importance of dominance, control, and achievement in men. These expectations can create a breeding ground for narcissistic behavior, as individuals strive to meet societal standards of success and power. Men who conform to these stereotypes may be more likely to exhibit narcissistic traits, as they seek validation and admiration from others.

7.1.2 Recognizing Male Narcissistic Traits

Identifying male narcissistic traits can be challenging, as they may be masked by societal expectations and cultural norms. However, there are certain red flags that can help individuals recognize potential narcissistic behavior in men. Some common traits include:

1. Grandiosity: A sense of superiority and entitlement, often accompanied by an inflated ego and a need for constant admiration.
2. Lack of empathy: Difficulty understanding or relating to the emotions and experiences of others.
3. Manipulative behavior: Using charm, flattery, and manipulation to control and exploit others for personal gain.
4. Exploitative tendencies: Taking advantage of others for personal benefit, without regard for their well-being.
5. Fragile self-esteem: A deep-seated insecurity that is masked by a grandiose facade, leading to a constant need for validation and praise.
6. Lack of accountability: Avoiding responsibility for one's actions and deflecting blame onto others.
7. Boundary violations: Disregarding the boundaries and needs of others, often crossing personal and emotional boundaries without remorse.

7.1.3 Challenges and Strategies for Dealing with Male Narcissists

Dealing with male narcissists can be particularly challenging due to societal expectations and power dynamics. However, there are strategies that can help individuals navigate these relationships more effectively:

1. Establish and maintain boundaries: Clearly define and communicate

your boundaries, and be firm in enforcing them. Narcissists often push boundaries, so it is crucial to stand your ground and protect your emotional well-being.

2. Practice self-care: Prioritize your own needs and well-being. Engage in activities that bring you joy and fulfillment, and surround yourself with a supportive network of friends and family.

3. Seek professional help: If you find yourself struggling to cope with a male narcissist in your life, consider seeking therapy or counseling. A mental health professional can provide guidance and support as you navigate the challenges of dealing with narcissistic individuals.

4. Educate yourself: Learn more about narcissistic personality styles and the tactics they employ. Understanding their behavior can help you develop strategies to protect yourself and maintain your emotional well-being.

5. Limit contact when necessary: If the relationship becomes toxic or abusive, it may be necessary to limit or cut off contact with the narcissistic individual. Your safety and well-being should always be the top priority.

7.1.4 Supporting Male Victims of Narcissistic Abuse

It is important to recognize that both men and women can be victims of narcissistic abuse. However, due to societal expectations and stereotypes, male victims may face unique challenges in seeking support and validation. Male victims of narcissistic abuse may feel ashamed or emasculated, as their experiences may contradict societal notions of masculinity.

To support male victims of narcissistic abuse, it is crucial to create a safe and non-judgmental space for them to share their experiences. Encourage open and honest communication, and validate their feelings and emotions. Offer resources and support networks that specifically cater to male victims of narcissistic abuse, as they may benefit from connecting with others who have had similar experiences.

By raising awareness and challenging societal expectations, we can create a more compassionate and understanding society that supports individuals of all genders in their journey to heal and recover from narcissistic abuse.

7.2 Recognizing Male Narcissistic Traits

When discussing narcissistic personality styles, it is important to recognize that narcissism can manifest differently in males compared to females. While both genders can exhibit narcissistic traits, societal expectations and cultural norms often shape the way these traits are expressed. Understanding the specific characteristics associated with male narcissism can help individuals identify and navigate relationships with male narcissists more effectively.

7.2.1 The Grandiose Sense of Self-Importance

One of the key traits commonly observed in male narcissists is an inflated sense of self-importance. They often believe they are superior to others and expect special treatment and admiration. This grandiose self-view can manifest in various ways, such as boasting about achievements, exaggerating their abilities, or seeking constant validation and praise.

7.2.2 Need for Constant Attention and Admiration

Male narcissists have an insatiable need for attention and admiration from others. They crave constant validation and seek out situations where they can be the center of attention. They may engage in attention-seeking behaviors, such as dominating conversations, interrupting others, or engaging in grandiose gestures to draw attention to themselves.

7.2.3 Lack of Empathy and Emotional Connection

Empathy and emotional connection are often lacking in male narcissists. They struggle to understand or relate to the emotions and experiences of others. Their self-centeredness and inability to empathize can lead to a disregard for the feelings and needs of those around them. Male narcissists may exploit others for personal gain without remorse or guilt.

7.2.4 Manipulative and Controlling Behavior

Male narcissists often exhibit manipulative and controlling behavior in their relationships. They may use tactics such as gaslighting, where they distort the truth to make their victims doubt their own perceptions and reality. They may also employ manipulation techniques to maintain power and control over their partners, friends, or colleagues.

7.2.5 Fragile Self-Esteem and Reactivity to Criticism

Despite their grandiose self-image, male narcissists often have fragile self-esteem. They are highly sensitive to criticism and may react with anger, defensiveness, or even aggression when their ego is threatened. This reactivity to criticism can make it challenging to have open and honest communication with them.

7.2.6 Exploitative and Entitled Behavior

Male narcissists often exhibit a sense of entitlement and a belief that they deserve special treatment. They may exploit others for personal gain, whether it be financial, emotional, or social. They may manipulate situations to their advantage and expect others to cater to their needs and desires without reciprocation.

7.2.7 Lack of Boundaries and Respect for Others

Respecting boundaries and the autonomy of others is not a priority for male narcissists. They may disregard personal boundaries, invade personal space, or manipulate others into doing things they are not comfortable with. This lack of respect for boundaries can lead to feelings of violation and discomfort in their relationships.

7.2.8 Difficulty in Maintaining Long-Term Relationships

Male narcissists often struggle to maintain long-term, healthy relationships. Their self-centeredness, lack of empathy, and manipulative behavior can create a toxic dynamic that is unsustainable in the long run. They may cycle through relationships, seeking new sources of validation and admiration when their current partner no longer meets their needs.

7.2.9 Variations in Severity and Presentations

It is important to note that narcissistic traits can vary in severity and presentation among individuals. Some male narcissists may exhibit more overt and aggressive behaviors, while others may display covert and subtle manipulation tactics. The severity of narcissistic traits can also range from mild to extreme, with more severe cases often leading to a diagnosis of Narcissistic Personality Disorder (NPD).

Understanding the variations in severity and presentations of male narcissistic traits can help individuals recognize and protect themselves from potential harm in their relationships.

Remember, recognizing these traits is the first step in protecting yourself from potential harm. If you suspect that you are in a relationship with a male narcissist, it is essential to prioritize your well-being and seek support from trusted friends, family, or professionals who can provide guidance and assistance.

7.3 Challenges and Strategies for Dealing with Male Narcissists

Dealing with male narcissists can present unique challenges due to societal expectations and gender dynamics. Understanding the traits and behaviors associated with male narcissism is crucial in developing effective strategies for dealing with them. In this section, we will explore the challenges faced when dealing with male narcissists and provide strategies to navigate these difficult relationships.

7.3.1 Recognizing Male Narcissistic Traits

Male narcissists often exhibit similar traits to their female counterparts, but societal expectations and gender roles can influence the way these traits are expressed. Some common traits of male narcissists include:

1. Grandiosity and entitlement: Male narcissists may have an inflated sense of self-importance and believe they are entitled to special treatment or privileges due to their gender.
2. Lack of empathy: They may struggle to understand or care about the feelings and needs of others, often prioritizing their own desires and goals.
3. Manipulation and control: Male narcissists may use manipulation tactics such as gaslighting, emotional blackmail, or coercion to maintain power and control in relationships.
4. Fragile self-esteem: Despite their outward confidence, male narcissists often have fragile self-esteem and are highly sensitive to criticism or perceived threats to their ego.
5. Exploitation of others: They may exploit others for personal gain, using charm and charisma to manipulate and take advantage of those around them.
6. Aggression and dominance: Male narcissists may display aggressive or dominant behaviors to assert their superiority and maintain control over others.

It is important to note that not all men exhibit these traits, and narcissism exists on a spectrum. However, recognizing these traits can help identify potential red flags and protect oneself from entering into harmful relationships.

7.3.2 Establishing Boundaries and Assertiveness

Dealing with male narcissists requires setting and enforcing clear boundaries. Establishing boundaries helps protect your emotional well-being and prevents the narcissist from manipulating or exploiting you. Here are some strategies for setting boundaries with male narcissists:

1. Clearly communicate your needs and expectations: Be assertive in expressing your boundaries and expectations. Use "I" statements to convey your feelings and needs, and be firm in your communication.
2. Practice self-care: Prioritize self-care and make time for activities that bring you joy and relaxation. Taking care of your own well-being is essential when dealing with a male narcissist.
3. Limit contact and exposure: If possible, minimize contact with the narcissist to reduce their influence and control over your life. Set boundaries around communication and interaction.
4. Seek support from trusted individuals: Reach out to friends, family, or support groups who can provide emotional support and guidance. Having a strong support network can help you navigate the challenges of dealing with a male narcissist.
5. Educate yourself about narcissism: Understanding the dynamics of narcissistic behavior can help you recognize manipulation tactics and develop effective strategies for dealing with them.

7.3.3 Seeking Professional Help

Dealing with a male narcissist can be emotionally draining and challenging. In some cases, seeking professional help may be necessary to navigate these difficult relationships. A therapist or counselor can provide guidance, support, and strategies for dealing with the specific challenges posed by male narcissists. They can help you develop coping mechanisms, improve your self-esteem, and explore healthy ways to manage the relationship or disengage from it if necessary.

7.3.4 Protecting Yourself from Male Narcissists

Prevention is always better than cure when it comes to dealing with male narcissists. Here are some strategies to protect yourself from getting involved in romantic relationships with male narcissists:

1. Trust your instincts: If something feels off or too good to be true, listen to your gut instincts. Pay attention to any red flags or warning signs early on in the relationship.
2. Take things slow: Allow the relationship to develop gradually. Rushing into a relationship can make it easier for a narcissist to manipulate and control you.
3. Look for consistent behavior: Observe how the person treats others, including friends, family, and colleagues. Consistent patterns of disrespectful or manipulative behavior may indicate narcissistic tendencies.
4. Seek feedback from trusted individuals: Share your concerns with friends or family members who can provide an objective perspective. They may notice red flags that you might have missed.
5. Set healthy boundaries: Establish and maintain your boundaries from the beginning of the relationship. A healthy partner will respect and honor your boundaries.

Remember, it is not your fault if you find yourself in a relationship with a male narcissist. Many people have experienced similar situations, and it is important to seek support and understanding from others who have been through similar experiences.

Dealing with male narcissists can be challenging, but by recognizing the traits, setting boundaries, seeking support, and protecting yourself, you can navigate these relationships with greater resilience and self-preservation.

7.4 Supporting Male Victims of Narcissistic Abuse

Supporting male victims of narcissistic abuse is crucial in helping them heal and regain their sense of self-worth and emotional well-being. While the focus of narcissistic abuse is often on female victims, it is important to recognize that males can also be targets of narcissistic individuals. In this section, we will explore the unique challenges faced by male victims and provide strategies for support and recovery.

7.4.1 Understanding the Dynamics of Narcissistic Abuse

Narcissistic abuse can have a profound impact on male victims, often leaving them feeling confused, isolated, and emotionally drained. It is important to understand the dynamics of narcissistic abuse to effectively support male victims. Narcissists manipulate and exploit their victims, using tactics such as gaslighting, emotional manipulation, and belittlement to maintain control and power over them.

Male victims of narcissistic abuse may face additional challenges due to societal expectations and stereotypes. Society often expects men to be strong, self-reliant, and unaffected by emotional abuse. This can make it difficult for male victims to recognize and seek help for the abuse they are experiencing.

7.4.2 Validating Male Victims' Experiences

One of the most important ways to support male victims of narcissistic abuse is to validate their experiences. Many male victims may struggle with self-doubt and self-blame, questioning whether they are overreacting or imagining the abuse. By acknowledging their experiences and validating their emotions, we can help male victims regain their sense of self and trust in their own perceptions.

It is crucial to emphasize that no one deserves to be abused, regardless of their gender. Male victims should be reminded that their experiences are valid and that seeking support is a sign of strength, not weakness.

7.4.3 Providing Emotional Support

Male victims of narcissistic abuse often face unique challenges when seeking emotional support. Traditional gender roles may discourage men from expressing vulnerability or seeking help. As a support system, it is important to create a safe and non-judgmental space for male victims to share their experiences and emotions.

Encourage male victims to express their feelings and validate their emotions. Active listening, empathy, and reassurance can go a long way in helping male victims feel heard and understood. Remind them that seeking professional help, such as therapy or support groups, is a valuable resource for healing and recovery.

7.4.4 Encouraging Self-Care and Self-Compassion

Male victims of narcissistic abuse often neglect their own needs and well-being while focusing on the needs of the narcissist. Encouraging self-care and self-compassion is essential in helping male victims rebuild their sense of self-worth and regain control over their lives.

Support male victims in developing self-care routines that prioritize their physical, emotional, and mental well-being. Encourage activities that promote relaxation, self-reflection, and personal growth. Remind them that self-compassion is not selfish but necessary for healing and moving forward.

7.4.5 Building a Support Network

Building a support network is crucial for male victims of narcissistic abuse. Encourage them to reach out to trusted friends, family members, or support groups who can provide understanding, validation, and guidance. Connecting with others who have experienced similar situations can be particularly beneficial, as they can offer empathy and share coping strategies.

Support male victims in setting boundaries with toxic individuals and surrounding themselves with positive and supportive people. Encourage them to seek professional help, such as therapy or counseling, to further explore their experiences and develop healthy coping mechanisms.

7.4.6 Empowering Male Victims to Take Action

Empowering male victims of narcissistic abuse involves helping them regain their sense of agency and control over their lives. Encourage them to set goals, both short-term and long-term, that align with their values and aspirations. Support them in taking steps towards their goals, whether it be seeking legal assistance, pursuing new hobbies, or exploring career opportunities.

It is important to remind male victims that they are not defined by their past experiences and that they have the power to create a fulfilling and healthy future. Encourage them to focus on personal growth, self-reflection, and self-improvement.

7.4.7 Spreading Awareness and Advocacy

Raising awareness about male victims of narcissistic abuse is crucial in breaking the stigma and providing support. Encourage male victims to share their stories, whether anonymously or publicly, to help others recognize and understand the signs of narcissistic abuse. By sharing their experiences, they can inspire and empower others who may be going through similar situations.

Advocacy efforts should also focus on educating society about the prevalence of narcissistic abuse in all genders. By challenging societal stereotypes and promoting empathy and understanding, we can create a safer and more supportive environment for all victims of narcissistic abuse.

Supporting male victims of narcissistic abuse requires empathy, understanding, and a commitment to breaking the silence surrounding this issue. By providing validation, emotional support, and practical guidance, we can help male victims heal, regain their self-worth, and move forward towards a brighter future.

8

Chapter 8

Understanding Narcissism in Females

8.1 Societal Stereotypes and Female Narcissism

Societal stereotypes play a significant role in shaping our understanding of narcissism. When it comes to narcissistic personality styles, the focus is often on male narcissists. However, it is essential to recognize that narcissism can manifest in both males and females. In this section, we will explore the societal stereotypes surrounding female narcissism and shed light on the unique challenges and perspectives associated with it.

8.1.1 Challenging Stereotypes

Society often portrays women as nurturing, empathetic, and selfless individuals. These stereotypes can make it challenging to recognize and acknowledge female narcissism. The expectation that women should be caring and compassionate can lead to the dismissal or misinterpretation of narcissistic traits in females.

It is crucial to understand that narcissism is not limited to any gender. Females can exhibit narcissistic traits just as males can. By challenging these

93

stereotypes, we can create a more accurate and inclusive understanding of narcissistic personality styles.

8.1.2 Recognizing Female Narcissistic Traits

To effectively identify and address female narcissism, it is essential to be aware of the common traits associated with this personality style. While the specific traits may vary from person to person, some characteristics are often observed in female narcissists:

1. **Grandiosity and entitlement:** Female narcissists may have an inflated sense of self-importance and believe they deserve special treatment and admiration.

2. **Lack of empathy:** Empathy deficit is a common trait in narcissistic individuals, including females. They may struggle to understand or care about the feelings and needs of others.

3. **Manipulation and control:** Female narcissists may employ manipulative tactics to maintain power and control in their relationships. They may use emotional manipulation, gaslighting, or other forms of psychological manipulation to assert dominance.

4. **Superficial charm:** Female narcissists can be charismatic and charming, especially during the initial stages of a relationship. They may use their charm to manipulate and exploit others for personal gain.

5. **Attention-seeking behavior:** Female narcissists often crave attention and validation from others. They may engage in attention-seeking behaviors, such as excessive self-promotion or dramatic displays, to ensure they remain the center of attention.

6. **Lack of accountability:** Female narcissists may struggle to take responsibility for their actions and may deflect blame onto others. They may refuse to acknowledge their mistakes or apologize genuinely.

8.1.3 Challenges and Strategies for Dealing with Female Narcissists

Navigating relationships with female narcissists can be particularly challenging due to societal expectations and stereotypes. Here are some strategies to help you cope with and manage interactions with female narcissists:

1. **Set boundaries:** Establish clear boundaries and communicate them assertively. Female narcissists may push boundaries, so it is crucial to be firm and consistent in enforcing them.
2. **Practice self-care:** Prioritize your emotional well-being and engage in self-care activities. Taking care of yourself will help you maintain your resilience and protect your mental health.
3. **Seek support:** Reach out to trusted friends, family, or support groups who can provide validation and guidance. Sharing your experiences with others who understand can be incredibly empowering.
4. **Educate yourself:** Learn more about narcissistic personality styles and female narcissism. Understanding the dynamics at play can help you navigate these relationships more effectively.

8.1.4 Supporting Female Victims of Narcissistic Abuse

It is essential to recognize that anyone, regardless of gender, can be a victim of narcissistic abuse. Supporting female victims of narcissistic abuse involves creating a safe and non-judgmental space for them to share their experiences. Here are some ways you can support female victims:

1. **Listen without judgment:** Offer a listening ear and validate their experiences. Avoid blaming or shaming them for their involvement in the relationship.
2. **Provide resources:** Share information about support groups, therapists, or helplines that specialize in narcissistic abuse. Encourage them to seek professional help if needed.
3. **Empowerment and validation:** Help them rebuild their self-esteem

and self-worth by providing validation and reminding them of their strengths and resilience.

4. **Encourage self-care:** Support them in prioritizing their well-being and engaging in self-care activities. Encourage them to explore hobbies, practice mindfulness, and engage in activities that bring them joy.

By challenging societal stereotypes and recognizing the presence of female narcissism, we can create a more comprehensive understanding of narcissistic personality styles. It is crucial to support both male and female victims of narcissistic abuse and work towards breaking the cycle of narcissism in our relationships and communities.

8.2 Recognizing Female Narcissistic Traits

Narcissistic personality styles can manifest in both males and females, and it is important to recognize and understand the specific traits associated with female narcissism. While the core characteristics of narcissism remain the same, there may be variations in the way these traits are expressed and presented in women. In this section, we will explore the distinct traits commonly observed in female narcissists and provide insights into recognizing and dealing with them.

8.2.1 The Mask of Charm and Empathy

Female narcissists often possess an uncanny ability to charm and manipulate others. They can be highly skilled at presenting themselves as caring, empathetic, and nurturing individuals. This charm is often used as a tool to gain control and admiration from those around them. They may appear to be the epitome of kindness and compassion, but underneath this facade lies a deep sense of entitlement and a need for constant validation.

8.2.2 Grandiosity and Superiority

Similar to their male counterparts, female narcissists exhibit grandiose and superiority complexes. They have an inflated sense of self-importance and believe they are unique and deserving of special treatment. They may constantly seek attention and admiration, often exaggerating their achievements and talents. Female narcissists may also engage in competitive behaviors, always striving to be the center of attention and outshine others.

8.2.3 Manipulation and Emotional Exploitation

Female narcissists are adept at manipulating others to serve their own needs and desires. They may use emotional manipulation tactics such as guilt-tripping, gaslighting, and playing the victim to control and dominate their relationships. They exploit the emotions and vulnerabilities of those around them, using them as tools to maintain their power and control.

8.2.4 Lack of Empathy and Emotional Connection

One of the defining traits of narcissism is a lack of empathy, and this holds true for female narcissists as well. They struggle to understand or connect with the emotions of others, often dismissing or invalidating them. Female narcissists may appear cold and indifferent to the feelings of those around them, prioritizing their own needs and desires above all else.

8.2.5 Envy and Jealousy

Female narcissists can be highly envious and jealous of others. They may feel threatened by the success or achievements of those around them and will go to great lengths to undermine or belittle them. This envy stems from their deep-seated insecurity and fear of being overshadowed or outshined by others.

8.2.6 Controlling and Manipulative Relationships

In romantic relationships, female narcissists often seek partners who can provide them with a constant source of admiration and validation. They may initially appear loving and attentive, but as the relationship progresses, their true narcissistic traits begin to surface. They may exert control over their partners, dictating their actions, isolating them from friends and family, and demanding unwavering loyalty.

8.2.7 Red Flags in Dating

When entering the dating world, it is crucial to be aware of the red flags that may indicate a potential partner with narcissistic traits. Some warning signs to look out for include:

- Excessive self-focus and self-promotion
- A sense of entitlement and superiority
- Lack of empathy and disregard for others' feelings
- Constant need for admiration and attention
- Manipulative and controlling behaviors
- Inconsistent or contradictory behavior
- Jealousy and possessiveness
- Difficulty accepting criticism or taking responsibility for their actions

8.2.8 Strategies for Dealing with Female Narcissists

Dealing with a female narcissist can be challenging, but there are strategies that can help navigate these relationships:

- Set and maintain clear boundaries: Establishing and enforcing boundaries is crucial when dealing with a female narcissist. Clearly communicate your limits and expectations, and be prepared to enforce consequences if they are crossed.

- Seek support: Reach out to trusted friends, family, or support groups who can provide guidance and understanding. Having a support system in place can help you navigate the challenges of dealing with a female narcissist.
- Practice self-care: Prioritize your own well-being and engage in activities that bring you joy and fulfillment. Taking care of yourself is essential when dealing with the emotional toll of a relationship with a female narcissist.
- Seek professional help if needed: If the relationship becomes emotionally or physically abusive, it is important to seek professional help. A therapist or counselor can provide guidance and support as you navigate the challenges of dealing with a female narcissist.

Recognizing and understanding the traits associated with female narcissism is crucial for protecting yourself and maintaining healthy relationships. By being aware of the red flags and implementing strategies for dealing with female narcissists, you can empower yourself to navigate these challenging dynamics and prioritize your own well-being. Remember, you are not alone, and many others have experienced similar relationships.

8.3 Challenges and Strategies for Dealing with Female Narcissists

Dealing with a female narcissist can present its own unique set of challenges. While narcissism is not limited to any gender, societal stereotypes and expectations often make it harder to recognize and address narcissistic traits in women. In this section, we will explore the challenges that come with dealing with female narcissists and provide strategies to navigate these difficult relationships.

8.3.1 Recognizing Female Narcissistic Traits

Recognizing narcissistic traits in women can be challenging due to societal expectations and stereotypes. Women are often expected to be nurturing, empathetic, and selfless, which can make it harder to identify narcissistic behaviors. However, it is important to remember that narcissism can manifest in both covert and overt ways in women, just as it does in men.

Some common traits of female narcissists include:

1. **Excessive need for attention**: Female narcissists often crave constant admiration and attention from others. They may go to great lengths to ensure they are the center of attention in social situations.
2. **Lack of empathy**: Empathy is a key characteristic that is often lacking in narcissistic individuals. Female narcissists may struggle to understand or care about the feelings and needs of others.
3. **Manipulative behavior**: Female narcissists are skilled manipulators who use charm, flattery, and manipulation tactics to control and exploit others for their own gain.
4. **Sense of entitlement**: Female narcissists often have an inflated sense of self-importance and believe they deserve special treatment and privileges.
5. **Lack of accountability**: Female narcissists rarely take responsibility for their actions and are quick to shift blame onto others. They may refuse to acknowledge their mistakes or apologize for their behavior.
6. **Superficial relationships**: Female narcissists tend to have shallow and transactional relationships. They may only be interested in others if they can provide them with attention, admiration, or resources.

8.3.2 Strategies for Dealing with Female Narcissists

Dealing with a female narcissist can be emotionally draining and challenging. However, there are strategies you can employ to protect yourself and navigate these difficult relationships:

1. **Set boundaries**: Establish clear boundaries and communicate them assertively. Female narcissists may try to push your boundaries, so it is important to be firm and consistent in enforcing them.

2. **Practice self-care**: Prioritize your own well-being and engage in activities that bring you joy and fulfillment. Taking care of yourself will help you maintain your emotional resilience when dealing with a female narcissist.

3. **Seek support**: Reach out to trusted friends, family members, or support groups who can provide you with emotional support and guidance. Sharing your experiences with others who understand can be validating and empowering.

4. **Educate yourself**: Learn more about narcissistic personality disorder and female narcissism. Understanding the underlying dynamics and behaviors can help you navigate the relationship more effectively.

5. **Avoid engaging in power struggles**: Female narcissists thrive on conflict and control. Refrain from engaging in power struggles or trying to change their behavior. Instead, focus on protecting yourself and setting healthy boundaries.

6. **Practice assertiveness**: Develop assertiveness skills to effectively communicate your needs and concerns. Be clear, direct, and confident in expressing yourself while maintaining respect for yourself and the other person.

7. **Document incidents**: Keep a record of any incidents or abusive behaviors. This documentation can be helpful if you need to seek legal or professional assistance in the future.

8. **Limit contact**: If possible, limit your contact with the female narcissist. Minimizing interactions can help protect your emotional well-being and reduce the negative impact of the relationship.

9. **Seek professional help**: If the relationship becomes too toxic or abusive, consider seeking professional help from a therapist or counselor who specializes in narcissistic abuse. They can provide guidance and support as you navigate the challenges of dealing with a female narcissist.

Remember, it is not your fault that you are in a relationship with a narcissist. Many people have fallen victim to their manipulative tactics. By recognizing the signs, setting boundaries, and seeking support, you can protect yourself and begin the journey towards healing and recovery.

Conclusion

Dealing with a female narcissist can be a challenging and emotionally draining experience. It is important to recognize the unique challenges that come with identifying and addressing narcissistic traits in women. By understanding the common traits of female narcissists and employing strategies to protect yourself, set boundaries, and seek support, you can navigate these difficult relationships with greater resilience and self-preservation. Remember, you are not alone, and there is help available to support you on your journey towards healing and recovery.

8.4 Supporting Female Victims of Narcissistic Abuse

Supporting female victims of narcissistic abuse is crucial in helping them heal and regain their sense of self-worth and empowerment. Narcissistic abuse can have devastating effects on a woman's mental, emotional, and physical well-being, making it essential to provide them with the necessary support and resources to navigate their healing journey. This section will explore various strategies and approaches to support female victims of narcissistic abuse.

8.4.1 Understanding the Dynamics of Narcissistic Abuse

Before delving into supporting female victims of narcissistic abuse, it is important to understand the dynamics of this type of abuse. Narcissistic abuse is characterized by a pattern of manipulative and controlling behaviors employed by individuals with narcissistic personality styles. These behaviors can include gaslighting, emotional manipulation, belittling, and isolation, among others. Female victims of narcissistic abuse often experience a range of emotions, including confusion, self-doubt, and a diminished sense of self-worth.

8.4.2 Creating a Safe and Supportive Environment

Creating a safe and supportive environment is crucial for female victims of narcissistic abuse to feel heard, validated, and understood. It is important to provide them with a non-judgmental space where they can express their emotions and share their experiences without fear of blame or shame. Active listening, empathy, and validation are essential in establishing trust and fostering healing.

8.4.3 Educating and Empowering Female Victims

Educating female victims of narcissistic abuse about the dynamics of narcissism and the impact it has on their lives can be empowering. By understanding the traits and behaviors associated with narcissistic personality styles, victims can gain clarity and validation for their experiences. Providing resources such as books, articles, and support groups can further empower them to take control of their healing journey.

8.4.4 Encouraging Self-Care and Self-Compassion

Self-care and self-compassion are vital components of healing for female victims of narcissistic abuse. Encouraging them to prioritize their well-being and engage in activities that bring them joy and relaxation can help restore their sense of self. Practicing self-compassion involves treating oneself with kindness and understanding, acknowledging that the abuse was not their fault, and allowing themselves to heal at their own pace.

8.4.5 Building a Support Network

Building a strong support network is crucial for female victims of narcissistic abuse. Encourage them to reach out to trusted friends, family members, or support groups who can provide emotional support and understanding. Connecting with others who have experienced similar situations can be particularly beneficial, as it creates a sense of community and validation.

8.4.6 Seeking Professional Help

In some cases, seeking professional help may be necessary for female victims of narcissistic abuse. Therapists or counselors experienced in trauma and abuse can provide specialized support and guidance throughout the healing process. They can help victims process their emotions, develop coping strategies, and rebuild their self-esteem.

8.4.7 Empowering Female Victims to Set Boundaries

Empowering female victims of narcissistic abuse to set and enforce boundaries is crucial for their healing and protection. Encourage them to identify their needs and communicate them assertively. Setting boundaries helps victims regain a sense of control over their lives and prevents further manipulation and abuse.

8.4.8 Providing Legal and Practical Support

In cases where legal action or practical support is necessary, it is important to guide female victims of narcissistic abuse through the process. This may involve connecting them with legal resources, helping them gather evidence, or assisting with practical matters such as finding safe housing or financial support.

8.4.9 Promoting Self-Empowerment and Growth

Supporting female victims of narcissistic abuse also involves promoting self-empowerment and growth. Encourage them to explore their passions, set goals, and pursue personal development. By focusing on their own growth and well-being, victims can reclaim their lives and move forward with strength and resilience.

8.4.10 Raising Awareness and Advocacy

Raising awareness about narcissistic abuse and advocating for change is essential in supporting female victims. Encourage victims to share their stories if they feel comfortable, as it can help break the silence surrounding narcissistic abuse and inspire others to seek help. Supporting organizations and initiatives that aim to educate the public and provide resources for victims can also make a significant impact.

Supporting female victims of narcissistic abuse requires a compassionate and understanding approach. By providing them with the necessary support, resources, and empowerment, we can help them heal, rebuild their lives, and thrive beyond the trauma. Remember, no one deserves to be abused, and every woman deserves to live a life free from the grip of narcissistic abuse.

9

Chapter 9

Understanding Narcissism in the GLBTQI Community

9.1 Unique Challenges and Perspectives

Living with or encountering narcissistic personality styles can present unique challenges and perspectives, particularly within the GLBTQI community. While narcissism can manifest in various ways, it is important to understand the specific dynamics and issues that may arise within this community. This section will explore these challenges and provide insights into navigating relationships, recognizing narcissistic traits, and supporting victims of narcissistic abuse within the GLBTQI community.

9.1.1 Understanding the GLBTQI Community

The GLBTQI community encompasses individuals who identify as gay, lesbian, bisexual, transgender, intersex, or queer. Within this diverse community, individuals may face additional challenges when dealing with narcissistic personality styles. It is crucial to recognize that narcissism can affect anyone, regardless of their sexual orientation or gender identity. However, the GLBTQI community may encounter unique dynamics and societal pressures that can exacerbate the impact of narcissistic relationships.

9.1.2 Navigating Narcissistic Relationships in the GLBTQI Community

Recognizing narcissistic traits in GLBTQI relationships is essential for maintaining emotional well-being. While the signs of narcissism may be similar across different communities, it is important to consider the specific challenges faced by individuals within the GLBTQI community. These challenges can include societal stereotypes, internalized homophobia or transphobia, and the fear of losing support networks.

In GLBTQI relationships, narcissistic partners may exploit these vulnerabilities, using them as leverage for control and manipulation. They may weaponize societal prejudices or use gaslighting techniques to undermine their partner's self-esteem. It is crucial for individuals within the GLBTQI community to be aware of these tactics and seek support from understanding friends, family, or professionals.

9.1.3 Supporting GLBTQI Victims of Narcissistic Abuse

Supporting victims of narcissistic abuse within the GLBTQI community requires a compassionate and inclusive approach. It is essential to create safe spaces where individuals can share their experiences without fear of judgment or discrimination. Recognizing the unique challenges faced by GLBTQI victims is crucial in providing effective support.

Support networks, both within the GLBTQI community and outside of it, can play a vital role in helping victims heal and recover. These networks can provide validation, understanding, and resources to assist individuals in rebuilding their lives. Encouraging victims to seek professional help, such as therapy or counseling, can also be instrumental in their healing journey.

9.1.4 Building Healthy Relationships within the GLBTQI Community

Building healthy relationships within the GLBTQI community involves fostering a culture of respect, empathy, and equality. It is important to challenge societal stereotypes and expectations that may perpetuate narcissistic dynamics. By promoting open communication, mutual support, and emotional vulnerability, individuals can create relationships that are based on trust and authenticity.

Developing self-awareness and self-love is also crucial in building healthy relationships. Understanding one's own worth and setting boundaries can help individuals avoid getting involved with narcissistic partners. By prioritizing their own well-being and seeking partners who demonstrate empathy and respect, individuals within the GLBTQI community can cultivate relationships that are nurturing and fulfilling.

In conclusion, understanding the unique challenges and perspectives of narcissistic personality styles within the GLBTQI community is essential for providing effective support and fostering healthy relationships. By recognizing the specific dynamics and societal pressures faced by individuals within this community, we can work towards breaking the cycle of narcissism and promoting emotional well-being for all.

9.2 Recognizing Narcissistic Traits in GLBTQI Relationships

Narcissistic personality styles can manifest in various ways within the GLBTQI community, just as they do in any other community. It is important to recognize these traits in order to protect oneself from potential harm and navigate relationships more effectively. In this section, we will explore the specific characteristics and red flags to look out for when identifying narcissistic traits in GLBTQI relationships.

9.2.1 Understanding Narcissistic Traits

Narcissistic traits can be observed in both overt and covert forms within the GLBTQI community. Overt narcissism is characterized by grandiosity, attention-seeking behavior, and a sense of entitlement. These individuals often display an exaggerated sense of self-importance and seek constant admiration from others. On the other hand, covert narcissism is more subtle and hidden. Covert narcissists may appear modest and self-effacing, but they still possess a deep need for validation and control.

It is important to note that narcissistic traits can vary in severity and presentation. Some individuals may exhibit only a few narcissistic traits, while others may display a full-blown narcissistic personality disorder. Understanding the range of narcissistic traits can help individuals identify and protect themselves from potential harm in GLBTQI relationships.

9.2.2 Red Flags in GLBTQI Relationships

When entering into a romantic relationship within the GLBTQI community, it is crucial to be aware of red flags that may indicate the presence of narcissistic traits. These red flags can include:

1. Excessive self-focus: Narcissistic individuals often prioritize their own needs and desires above those of their partners. They may consistently steer conversations back to themselves and show little interest in their partner's experiences or emotions.
2. Lack of empathy: Empathy is a fundamental component of healthy relationships. Narcissistic individuals may struggle to understand or validate their partner's feelings, often dismissing or minimizing their emotions.
3. Manipulative behavior: Narcissists are skilled manipulators and may use tactics such as gaslighting, guilt-tripping, or emotional blackmail to control their partners. They may also engage in love-bombing, showering their partners with affection and attention in the early stages

of the relationship, only to withdraw it later.

4. Constant need for validation: Narcissistic individuals have an insatiable need for admiration and validation. They may constantly seek external validation from their partners, friends, or social media, and become easily threatened by any perceived criticism or rejection.

5. Boundary violations: Narcissists often have difficulty respecting boundaries and may invade their partner's personal space, privacy, or emotional boundaries. They may also exhibit possessive or controlling behavior, isolating their partners from friends and family.

6. Lack of accountability: Narcissistic individuals rarely take responsibility for their actions or admit when they are wrong. They may deflect blame onto others or make excuses for their behavior, making it challenging to resolve conflicts or address issues within the relationship.

9.2.3 Navigating GLBTQI Relationships with Narcissists

If you find yourself in a relationship with a narcissistic individual within the GLBTQI community, it is essential to prioritize your well-being and safety. Here are some strategies for navigating these relationships:

1. Establish and maintain boundaries: Clearly communicate your boundaries and expectations within the relationship. It is crucial to assertively enforce these boundaries and seek support from trusted friends or professionals if they are repeatedly violated.

2. Seek support: Reach out to friends, family, or support groups within the GLBTQI community who can provide understanding and guidance. Sharing your experiences with others who have faced similar challenges can be validating and empowering.

3. Practice self-care: Engage in activities that promote your physical, emotional, and mental well-being. This can include exercise, therapy, meditation, or pursuing hobbies and interests that bring you joy and fulfillment.

4. Educate yourself: Learn more about narcissistic personality styles and

the impact they can have on relationships. Understanding the dynamics at play can help you navigate the challenges more effectively and make informed decisions about your future.

9.2.4 Building Healthy Relationships within the GLBTQI Community

While it is important to be aware of narcissistic traits and protect oneself from potential harm, it is equally important to remember that not all relationships within the GLBTQI community are narcissistic. Building healthy relationships is possible and can be achieved by:

1. Self-reflection: Take the time to reflect on your own values, needs, and desires in a relationship. Understanding yourself better will enable you to make conscious choices and attract partners who align with your values.
2. Communication and mutual respect: Open and honest communication is the foundation of any healthy relationship. Ensure that both you and your partner feel heard, respected, and valued.
3. Emotional intelligence: Cultivate emotional intelligence by developing empathy, active listening skills, and the ability to regulate your own emotions. These skills will contribute to healthier and more fulfilling relationships.
4. Seek professional help if needed: If you find yourself repeatedly attracting narcissistic partners or struggling to maintain healthy relationships, consider seeking therapy or counseling. A mental health professional can provide guidance and support as you navigate the complexities of relationships.

Remember, recognizing narcissistic traits in GLBTQI relationships is crucial for self-protection and well-being. By being aware of red flags, setting boundaries, seeking support, and building healthy relationship patterns, you can create a fulfilling and authentic connection within the GLBTQI community.

9.3 Supporting GLBTQI Victims of Narcissistic Abuse

Supporting GLBTQI (gay, lesbian, bisexual, transgender, intersex, and queer) individuals who have experienced narcissistic abuse is crucial in helping them heal and regain their sense of self-worth. Narcissistic abuse can have a profound impact on anyone, regardless of their sexual orientation or gender identity. However, members of the GLBTQI community may face unique challenges and require specific support systems to navigate their healing journey. This section will explore the ways in which we can support GLBTQI victims of narcissistic abuse and help them rebuild their lives.

9.3.1 Understanding the Unique Challenges

GLBTQI individuals who have experienced narcissistic abuse may face additional challenges due to societal attitudes, discrimination, and the intersectionality of their identities. It is essential to acknowledge and understand these challenges to provide effective support. Some of the unique challenges faced by GLBTQI victims of narcissistic abuse include:

9.3.1.1 Stigma and Isolation

GLBTQI individuals may already face stigma and discrimination in society, which can be exacerbated when they are in a relationship with a narcissist. The fear of being judged or not being believed may prevent them from seeking help or disclosing their experiences. It is crucial to create a safe and non-judgmental environment where they feel comfortable sharing their stories.

9.3.1.2 Intersectionality

The intersectionality of sexual orientation, gender identity, and narcissistic abuse can complicate the healing process. GLBTQI individuals may struggle with reconciling their identities and experiences, leading to feelings of confusion, self-doubt, and internalized shame. It is important to provide support that acknowledges and respects their unique experiences and identities.

9.3.1.3 Lack of Resources

GLBTQI individuals may face a scarcity of resources specifically tailored to their needs. This can include a lack of support groups, therapists, or organizations that understand the intersection of their identities and the dynamics of narcissistic abuse. It is crucial to advocate for and create inclusive resources that address the specific challenges faced by GLBTQI victims.

9.3.2 Providing Support and Validation

Supporting GLBTQI victims of narcissistic abuse involves providing a safe and validating space where they can heal and rebuild their lives. Here are some ways in which we can offer support:

9.3.2.1 Creating Safe Spaces

Creating safe spaces where GLBTQI individuals can share their experiences without fear of judgment or discrimination is essential. This can be done through support groups, online forums, or LGBTQ+ community centers. These spaces should be inclusive, affirming, and sensitive to the unique challenges faced by GLBTQI victims of narcissistic abuse.

9.3.2.2 Validation and Empathy

Validating the experiences of GLBTQI victims is crucial in helping them heal. Many individuals who have experienced narcissistic abuse may doubt their own perceptions and feelings due to gaslighting and manipulation. Offering empathy, validation, and reassurance can help them regain their sense of self and trust in their own experiences.

9.3.2.3 Cultivating Resilience and Empowerment

Supporting GLBTQI victims of narcissistic abuse involves empowering them to reclaim their lives and build resilience. This can be done through providing resources on self-care, self-compassion, and self-empowerment. Encouraging them to engage in activities that promote healing, such as therapy, mindfulness, and creative outlets, can also be beneficial.

9.3.3 Addressing Intersectionality and Advocacy

Recognizing the intersectionality of GLBTQI identities and narcissistic abuse is crucial in providing effective support. Here are some ways in which we can address intersectionality and advocate for GLBTQI victims:

9.3.3.1 Education and Awareness

Raising awareness about the unique challenges faced by GLBTQI victims of narcissistic abuse is essential. This can be done through educational campaigns, workshops, and community events. By increasing awareness, we can reduce stigma, promote understanding, and encourage individuals to seek help.

9.3.3.2 Collaboration with LGBTQ+ Organizations

Collaborating with LGBTQ+ organizations and community centers can help create a network of support for GLBTQI victims of narcissistic abuse. By working together, we can ensure that resources and services are inclusive, accessible, and tailored to the specific needs of the community.

9.3.3.3 Advocacy for Policy Changes

Advocating for policy changes that protect the rights and well-being of GLBTQI individuals is crucial. This can include advocating for laws that address discrimination, promote inclusive healthcare, and provide legal protections for victims of narcissistic abuse. By advocating for change, we can create a more supportive and inclusive society for GLBTQI victims.

9.3.4 Building Healthy Relationships within the GLBTQI Community

Building healthy relationships within the GLBTQI community is essential for the well-being and healing of individuals who have experienced narcissistic abuse. Here are some strategies for fostering healthy relationships:

9.3.4.1 Education and Awareness

Promoting education and awareness about healthy relationship dynamics within the GLBTQI community is crucial. This can be done through workshops, community discussions, and online resources. By providing information on red flags, healthy communication, and boundaries, we can empower individuals to make informed choices in their relationships.

9.3.4.2 Supportive Networks

Encouraging the development of supportive networks within the GLBTQI community can provide a sense of belonging and support. This can be done through social events, support groups, or online platforms. By fostering connections and support, individuals can find validation, understanding, and healthy relationship models.

9.3.4.3 Role Models and Mentorship

Promoting positive role models and mentorship within the GLBTQI community can provide guidance and support for individuals seeking healthy relationships. By connecting individuals with mentors who have experienced healthy relationships, we can provide guidance, encouragement, and inspiration.

Supporting GLBTQI victims of narcissistic abuse requires a comprehensive understanding of the unique challenges they face. By creating safe spaces, providing validation and support, addressing intersectionality, and promoting healthy relationships, we can empower GLBTQI individuals to heal, thrive, and build fulfilling lives beyond narcissistic abuse.

10

Chapter 10

Empowering Yourself

10.1 Assertiveness Training

Assertiveness is a crucial skill when dealing with individuals who exhibit narcissistic personality styles. It allows you to communicate effectively, set boundaries, and protect your emotional well-being. In this section, we will explore assertiveness training techniques that can empower you to navigate relationships with narcissists more effectively.

10.1.1 Understanding Assertiveness

Assertiveness is the ability to express your thoughts, feelings, and needs in a direct and respectful manner, while also considering the rights and boundaries of others. It involves standing up for yourself, expressing your opinions, and setting clear boundaries without being aggressive or passive.

When dealing with narcissistic individuals, assertiveness is particularly important. They often manipulate and exploit others, taking advantage of their passive or aggressive tendencies. By developing assertiveness skills, you can protect yourself from their tactics and maintain your self-worth.

10.1.2 The Importance of Effective Communication

Effective communication is the foundation of assertiveness. It involves expressing yourself clearly, listening actively, and understanding the perspectives of others. When dealing with narcissists, it is essential to communicate your needs and boundaries assertively, as they may attempt to dismiss or invalidate your feelings.

To communicate effectively with narcissists, consider the following tips:

1. Use "I" statements: Start your sentences with "I" to express your feelings and needs without blaming or attacking the other person. For example, say, "I feel hurt when you dismiss my opinions" instead of "You always ignore me."
2. Be specific and concise: Clearly state your concerns or requests in a straightforward manner. Narcissists may try to divert the conversation or confuse you, so it is important to stay focused and concise.
3. Maintain a calm and composed demeanor: Narcissists often thrive on emotional reactions. By remaining calm and composed, you can prevent them from manipulating your emotions and maintain control of the conversation.
4. Use active listening: Show genuine interest in what the narcissist is saying, but also ensure that they reciprocate by listening to you. Reflect back their statements to demonstrate that you understand their perspective, but also assert your own thoughts and feelings.

10.1.3 Setting Boundaries

Setting boundaries is a crucial aspect of assertiveness when dealing with narcissistic individuals. Narcissists often lack empathy and disregard the boundaries of others. By establishing clear boundaries, you can protect yourself from their manipulative behaviors and maintain your emotional well-being.

Consider the following strategies for setting boundaries with narcissists:

1. Identify your limits: Reflect on your values, needs, and emotional well-being to determine what boundaries are important to you. This will help you establish clear guidelines for your interactions with narcissistic individuals.

2. Communicate your boundaries assertively: Clearly express your boundaries to the narcissist, using "I" statements and maintaining a calm demeanor. Be firm and consistent in enforcing these boundaries, even if they try to push back or manipulate you.

3. Be prepared for resistance: Narcissists may resist or disregard your boundaries, as they are accustomed to having control over others. Stay firm and remind yourself that your boundaries are essential for your well-being.

4. Seek support: It can be challenging to set and maintain boundaries with narcissists, especially if you have been conditioned to prioritize their needs. Seek support from trusted friends, family, or therapists who can provide guidance and encouragement.

10.1.4 Dealing with Manipulation and Gaslighting

Narcissists are skilled manipulators who often employ gaslighting techniques to undermine your perception of reality. Gaslighting involves distorting or denying your experiences, making you doubt your own sanity or memory. Assertiveness is crucial in countering these manipulative tactics.

Consider the following strategies when dealing with manipulation and gaslighting:

1. Trust your instincts: Narcissists may try to convince you that your feelings or perceptions are invalid. Trust your instincts and rely on your own judgment to maintain a clear understanding of reality.

2. Document incidents: Keep a record of incidents where the narcissist manipulates or gaslights you. This documentation can serve as a reminder of the truth and help you maintain your assertiveness when confronted with their tactics.

3. Seek validation from others: Reach out to trusted friends, family, or support groups who can provide validation and support. Their perspectives can help you maintain your confidence and assertiveness in the face of gaslighting.

4. Practice self-care: Engage in activities that promote self-care and emotional well-being. This can include practicing mindfulness, engaging in hobbies, or seeking therapy. Taking care of yourself strengthens your resilience and assertiveness.

Remember, assertiveness is a skill that can be developed and strengthened over time. By practicing effective communication, setting boundaries, and countering manipulation, you can empower yourself to navigate relationships with narcissistic individuals more effectively.

10.2 Cognitive Behavioral Techniques

Cognitive Behavioral Techniques (CBT) are powerful tools that can help individuals challenge and change negative thoughts and behaviors associated with narcissistic personality styles. By understanding and addressing these cognitive distortions, individuals can gain a greater sense of control over their thoughts and emotions, leading to improved mental well-being and healthier relationships. In this section, we will explore some key cognitive behavioral techniques that can be used to challenge negative thoughts and promote personal growth and healing.

10.2.1 Identifying Cognitive Distortions

One of the first steps in cognitive behavioral therapy is to identify and challenge cognitive distortions. These distortions are irrational and negative thoughts that contribute to feelings of low self-worth, self-blame, and emotional distress. By recognizing these distortions, individuals can begin to question their validity and replace them with more realistic and positive thoughts.

Some common cognitive distortions associated with narcissistic personality styles include:

1. **All-or-Nothing Thinking**: This distortion involves seeing things in black and white, with no room for shades of gray. Individuals may believe that they are either perfect or a complete failure, disregarding any middle ground.

2. **Overgeneralization**: This distortion involves making sweeping conclusions based on a single event or experience. For example, if a person with a narcissistic personality style experiences rejection in one relationship, they may believe that they are unlovable and will always be rejected.

3. **Personalization**: This distortion involves taking responsibility for events or situations that are beyond one's control. Individuals with narcissistic traits may blame themselves for the actions or behaviors of others, even when they are not at fault.

4. **Catastrophizing**: This distortion involves blowing things out of proportion and imagining the worst-case scenario. Individuals may exaggerate the consequences of their actions or believe that minor setbacks are catastrophic failures.

5. **Mind Reading**: This distortion involves assuming that one knows what others are thinking or feeling, without any evidence to support these assumptions. Individuals with narcissistic traits may believe that others are constantly judging or criticizing them, leading to feelings of insecurity and defensiveness.

10.2.2 Challenging Negative Thoughts

Once cognitive distortions have been identified, the next step is to challenge and replace them with more realistic and positive thoughts. This process involves examining the evidence for and against these negative thoughts and considering alternative explanations or perspectives.

Here are some techniques that can be used to challenge negative thoughts associated with narcissistic personality styles:

1. **Evidence Evaluation**: Encourage individuals to critically evaluate the evidence for their negative thoughts. Are there any facts or objective evidence that support these thoughts? Are there any alternative explanations or interpretations?

2. **Reality Testing**: Encourage individuals to seek feedback from trusted friends, family members, or professionals to gain a more balanced perspective. This can help challenge distorted beliefs and provide a more accurate understanding of oneself and others.

3. **Cognitive Restructuring**: Help individuals reframe their negative thoughts into more positive and realistic ones. This involves replacing negative self-talk with affirmations and statements that promote self-compassion and self-acceptance.

4. **Behavioral Experiments**: Encourage individuals to test their negative thoughts by engaging in behaviors that challenge them. For example, if someone believes they are unlovable, they can engage in activities that promote self-care and self-love to challenge this belief.

10.2.3 Developing Coping Strategies

In addition to challenging negative thoughts, it is important to develop effective coping strategies to manage the emotional distress associated with narcissistic personality styles. Here are some techniques that can be helpful:

1. **Emotion Regulation**: Teach individuals techniques for managing and regulating their emotions, such as deep breathing exercises, mindfulness meditation, and journaling. These techniques can help individuals become more aware of their emotions and develop healthier ways of coping with them.

2. **Problem-Solving Skills**: Help individuals develop problem-solving skills to address the challenges and conflicts that may arise in relationships. This involves identifying the problem, generating possible solutions, evaluating the pros and cons of each solution, and implementing the most effective one.

3. **Assertiveness Training**: Teach individuals assertiveness skills to express their needs, wants, and boundaries in a clear and respectful manner. This can help individuals establish healthy boundaries and communicate effectively with others.

4. **Self-Care Practices**: Encourage individuals to prioritize self-care activities that promote their physical, emotional, and mental well-being. This can include activities such as exercise, healthy eating, getting enough sleep, engaging in hobbies, and spending time with supportive friends and family.

By incorporating these cognitive behavioral techniques into their lives, individuals can begin to challenge negative thoughts, develop healthier coping strategies, and cultivate a greater sense of self-worth and resilience. It is important to remember that healing from the impact of narcissistic personality styles takes time and effort, but with the right tools and support, individuals can empower themselves to create a brighter and more fulfilling future.

10.3 Mindfulness and Self-Reflection

In the journey of understanding and surviving narcissistic personality styles, it is crucial to cultivate inner strength and resilience. Mindfulness and self-reflection are powerful tools that can help individuals navigate the complexities of dealing with narcissists and promote personal growth and healing. By developing these practices, individuals can gain a deeper understanding of themselves, their emotions, and their boundaries, enabling them to protect their well-being and establish healthier relationships.

10.3.1 The Power of Mindfulness

Mindfulness is the practice of being fully present in the moment, without judgment or attachment to thoughts or emotions. It involves paying attention to one's thoughts, feelings, and bodily sensations, allowing for a deeper understanding of oneself and the world around them. By cultivating mindfulness, individuals can develop a greater sense of self-awareness and emotional regulation, which are essential when dealing with narcissistic personality styles.

Practicing mindfulness can help individuals recognize and detach from the manipulative tactics often employed by narcissists. By observing their thoughts and emotions without getting caught up in them, individuals can maintain a sense of clarity and objectivity, making it easier to identify and respond to narcissistic behaviors effectively. Mindfulness also promotes self-compassion, allowing individuals to validate their experiences and emotions without self-blame or judgment.

10.3.2 Self-Reflection for Personal Growth

Self-reflection is a process of introspection and examination of one's thoughts, emotions, and behaviors. It involves taking the time to explore one's values, beliefs, and boundaries, and how they may have been influenced by past experiences with narcissistic individuals. Self-reflection allows individuals to gain insight into their own patterns and triggers, empowering them to make conscious choices and establish healthier boundaries in future relationships.

Engaging in self-reflection can help individuals identify any unresolved emotional wounds caused by narcissistic abuse. By acknowledging and processing these wounds, individuals can begin the healing process and work towards rebuilding their self-esteem and self-worth. Self-reflection also enables individuals to recognize any codependent tendencies or patterns of enabling, empowering them to break free from unhealthy relationship dynamics.

10.3.3 Cultivating Inner Strength

Mindfulness and self-reflection are powerful tools for cultivating inner strength and resilience. By practicing mindfulness, individuals can develop a greater sense of self-compassion and self-acceptance, recognizing that they are not to blame for the narcissist's behavior. This understanding allows individuals to let go of any feelings of guilt or shame and focus on their own healing and growth.

Self-reflection also helps individuals identify their strengths and values, enabling them to build a solid foundation of self-esteem and self-worth. By recognizing their own worth and setting healthy boundaries, individuals can protect themselves from further narcissistic abuse and establish fulfilling relationships based on mutual respect and empathy.

10.3.4 Incorporating Mindfulness and Self-Reflection into Daily Life

Incorporating mindfulness and self-reflection into daily life requires commitment and practice. Here are some strategies to help individuals cultivate these practices:

1. **Mindful Breathing**: Take a few moments each day to focus on your breath. Pay attention to the sensation of the breath entering and leaving your body, allowing yourself to become fully present in the moment.
2. **Journaling**: Set aside time each day to write down your thoughts, emotions, and reflections. Use this as an opportunity to explore your experiences and gain insight into your own patterns and triggers.
3. **Body Scan Meditation**: Practice a body scan meditation, where you systematically bring awareness to each part of your body, noticing any sensations or areas of tension. This practice can help you connect with your body and release any stored emotions or stress.
4. **Gratitude Practice**: Cultivate a daily gratitude practice by reflecting on three things you are grateful for each day. This practice can help shift your focus towards the positive aspects of your life and foster a

sense of appreciation.

5. **Seek Support**: Consider joining a support group or seeking therapy to further explore your experiences and emotions. Connecting with others who have gone through similar experiences can provide validation, support, and guidance on your healing journey.

Remember, mindfulness and self-reflection are ongoing practices that require patience and self-compassion. By incorporating these practices into your daily life, you can cultivate inner strength, promote healing, and establish healthier relationships moving forward.

Conclusion

Mindfulness and self-reflection are essential tools for individuals seeking to understand and survive narcissistic personality styles. By developing these practices, individuals can gain a deeper understanding of themselves, their emotions, and their boundaries, enabling them to protect their well-being and establish healthier relationships. Through mindfulness, individuals can detach from manipulative tactics and maintain clarity when dealing with narcissists. Self-reflection promotes personal growth, healing, and the establishment of healthier boundaries. By incorporating mindfulness and self-reflection into daily life, individuals can cultivate inner strength, resilience, and a greater sense of self-worth. Remember, these practices require commitment and patience, but they are powerful tools that can empower individuals to thrive beyond narcissistic abuse.

10.4 Self-Compassion and Forgiveness

Self-compassion and forgiveness are essential components of healing and recovering from the effects of narcissistic personality styles. When we have been in relationships with narcissists, it is common to blame ourselves and carry a heavy burden of guilt and shame. However, it is important to understand that we are not to blame for the narcissist's behavior. Many people have experienced relationships with narcissists, and it is not a reflection of our worth or character.

10.4.1 Cultivating Self-Compassion

Self-compassion involves treating ourselves with kindness, understanding, and acceptance, especially during difficult times. It is about acknowledging our pain and suffering without judgment and offering ourselves the same compassion we would extend to a loved one. Here are some strategies to cultivate self-compassion:

1. **Practice self-care**: Engage in activities that bring you joy and nourish your well-being. This could include hobbies, exercise, spending time in nature, or practicing mindfulness.
2. **Challenge self-critical thoughts**: Notice when you are being self-critical and replace those thoughts with kind and supportive ones. Remind yourself that you deserve love, respect, and understanding.
3. **Seek support**: Surround yourself with a supportive network of friends, family, or a therapist who can provide validation and empathy. Sharing your experiences with others who understand can be incredibly healing.
4. **Practice self-acceptance**: Embrace your strengths and weaknesses, accepting yourself as a whole person. Remember that nobody is perfect, and it is okay to make mistakes.
5. **Set boundaries**: Establish clear boundaries to protect yourself from further harm. This includes setting limits on how much contact you have with the narcissist and prioritizing your own well-being.

10.4.2 The Power of Forgiveness

Forgiveness is a powerful tool for healing, but it is important to note that forgiveness does not mean condoning or forgetting the narcissist's actions. Instead, forgiveness is a process of letting go of anger, resentment, and the desire for revenge. It is about freeing ourselves from the emotional burden and reclaiming our own happiness. Here are some steps to foster forgiveness:

1. **Acknowledge your pain**: Allow yourself to feel the pain and anger caused by the narcissist's actions. It is essential to validate your emotions and give yourself permission to heal.

2. **Understand the narcissist's limitations**: Recognize that narcissists have their own wounds and insecurities that drive their behavior. This understanding can help you detach emotionally and view their actions with compassion.

3. **Release expectations**: Let go of any expectations for an apology or acknowledgment from the narcissist. Accept that you may never receive the closure you desire and focus on your own healing instead.

4. **Focus on your growth**: Shift your focus from the narcissist to your own personal growth and well-being. Invest your energy in activities that bring you joy and help you move forward.

5. **Practice empathy**: Cultivate empathy towards yourself and the narcissist. This does not mean excusing their behavior but rather understanding the factors that contributed to their personality style.

6. **Seek professional help if needed**: If forgiveness feels challenging, consider seeking therapy or counseling to guide you through the process. A trained professional can provide support and help you navigate your emotions.

Remember, forgiveness is a personal journey, and it may take time. Be patient with yourself and celebrate each step forward, no matter how small.

Conclusion

Self-compassion and forgiveness are vital aspects of healing and recovering from the effects of narcissistic personality styles. By cultivating self-compassion, we can learn to treat ourselves with kindness and understanding, letting go of self-blame and embracing our worth. Forgiveness, on the other hand, allows us to release the emotional burden and reclaim our happiness.

It is a process of letting go of anger and resentment, focusing on our growth and well-being. Remember, healing takes time, and it is essential to be patient and gentle with ourselves throughout the journey.

11

Chapter 11

Moving Forward

11.1 Rebuilding Trust in Relationships

Rebuilding trust in relationships after experiencing narcissistic abuse can be a challenging and complex process. The manipulative and exploitative behaviors of narcissists can leave lasting emotional scars and make it difficult to trust others again. However, with time, self-reflection, and support, it is possible to heal and develop healthy relationships built on trust and authenticity.

Understanding the Impact of Narcissistic Abuse on Trust

Narcissistic abuse can have a profound impact on an individual's ability to trust others. The constant manipulation, gaslighting, and emotional manipulation employed by narcissists can erode one's sense of self and create a deep-seated fear of being vulnerable again. It is important to recognize that these feelings are a natural response to the trauma experienced and that healing takes time.

Self-Reflection and Healing

Before entering into new relationships, it is crucial to engage in self-reflection and healing. Take the time to understand the patterns and dynamics that led to the involvement with a narcissist. This self-awareness can help identify any vulnerabilities or codependent tendencies that may have attracted a narcissistic partner in the past.

Therapy can be a valuable tool in this healing process. A qualified therapist can provide guidance and support as you navigate the complex emotions and challenges associated with rebuilding trust. They can help you develop healthy coping mechanisms, set boundaries, and identify red flags in potential partners.

Setting Boundaries and Communicating Needs

Rebuilding trust starts with setting clear boundaries and effectively communicating your needs and expectations in relationships. It is essential to establish a strong sense of self and assertiveness to protect yourself from future harm. Learning to say no, expressing your feelings, and setting limits are crucial skills in maintaining healthy relationships.

Taking Time to Heal

It is important to give yourself time to heal before entering into new relationships. Rushing into a new romance without fully processing the trauma of narcissistic abuse can lead to repeating the same patterns. Take the time to focus on self-care, self-love, and rebuilding your self-esteem. Engage in activities that bring you joy, surround yourself with supportive friends and family, and practice self-compassion.

Building Trust in New Relationships

When entering into new relationships, it is natural to feel cautious and guarded. However, it is important not to let the actions of a narcissist define your future relationships. Here are some strategies to help rebuild trust:

1. Take it Slow: Allow the relationship to develop gradually. Take the time to get to know the person and observe their actions and behaviors over time.
2. Open Communication: Be open and honest about your past experiences with narcissistic abuse. Share your concerns and fears with your partner, allowing them to understand your needs and support you.
3. Consistency and Reliability: Look for consistent and reliable behavior in your partner. Trust is built through consistent actions and words that align.
4. Mutual Respect: Ensure that your partner respects your boundaries, opinions, and autonomy. Healthy relationships are built on mutual respect and equality.
5. Seek Support: Lean on your support network during this process. Share your experiences and concerns with trusted friends or a therapist who can provide guidance and reassurance.

Letting Go

Rebuilding trust also involves forgiving yourself for any perceived mistakes or shortcomings in past relationships. It is important to remember that narcissistic abuse is not your fault. Narcissists are skilled manipulators who prey on vulnerabilities. By practicing self-compassion and forgiveness, you can release any lingering guilt or self-blame and move forward with a renewed sense of self-worth.

Remember, rebuilding trust takes time and patience. It is a journey of self-discovery and growth. By prioritizing your well-being, setting boundaries, and surrounding yourself with supportive individuals, you can create a future filled with healthy, fulfilling relationships built on trust and authenticity.

11.2 Creating a Life of Authenticity and Fulfillment

Recovering from narcissistic abuse is a challenging journey, but it is also an opportunity for personal growth and transformation. After enduring the manipulations and emotional turmoil inflicted by a narcissistic personality, it is crucial to focus on rebuilding your life and creating a future filled with authenticity and fulfillment. This chapter will guide you through the process of reclaiming your sense of self, finding meaning and purpose, and thriving beyond the narcissistic experience.

11.2.1 Rediscovering Your Authentic Self

One of the most significant challenges faced by survivors of narcissistic abuse is reconnecting with their authentic selves. Narcissists often manipulate and control their victims, causing them to lose touch with their own desires, values, and aspirations. To create a life of authenticity and fulfillment, it is essential to embark on a journey of self-discovery.

Start by exploring your interests, passions, and values. Engage in activities that bring you joy and allow you to express your true self. Surround yourself with supportive and nurturing individuals who encourage your personal growth. As you reconnect with your authentic self, you will gain a deeper understanding of your needs and desires, paving the way for a more fulfilling life.

11.2.2 Setting Meaningful Goals

Setting meaningful goals is an integral part of creating a life of authenticity and fulfillment. After enduring the trauma of narcissistic abuse, it is crucial to establish goals that align with your values and aspirations. Take the time to reflect on what truly matters to you and what you want to achieve in various areas of your life, such as relationships, career, and personal growth.

When setting goals, ensure they are realistic, attainable, and in line with your values. Break them down into smaller, manageable steps to maintain motivation and track your progress. Celebrate each milestone you achieve, no matter how small, as it signifies your growth and resilience.

11.2.3 Cultivating Healthy Relationships

Rebuilding trust and establishing healthy relationships is a vital aspect of creating a fulfilling life after narcissistic abuse. Surround yourself with individuals who respect and value you for who you are. Seek out supportive friends, family members, or support groups who understand your experiences and can provide a safe space for healing and growth.

When entering new romantic relationships, it is crucial to be aware of the red flags associated with narcissistic personality styles. Look out for excessive self-centeredness, a lack of empathy, and a constant need for admiration. Trust your instincts and take your time getting to know potential partners before fully committing. Remember, you deserve a loving and healthy relationship built on mutual respect and trust.

11.2.4 Embracing Self-Care and Well-being

Prioritizing self-care and well-being is essential for creating a life of authenticity and fulfillment. After experiencing narcissistic abuse, it is crucial to nurture your physical, emotional, and mental well-being. Engage in activities that promote relaxation, such as meditation, yoga, or spending time in nature. Practice self-compassion and forgiveness, allowing yourself to heal from past wounds.

Take care of your physical health by maintaining a balanced diet, exercising regularly, and getting enough restful sleep. Seek professional help if needed, such as therapy or counseling, to address any lingering emotional or psychological effects of the abuse. Remember, self-care is not selfish; it is a necessary component of your healing journey.

11.2.5 Finding Meaning and Purpose

Finding meaning and purpose beyond the narcissistic experience is a powerful way to reclaim your life and create a fulfilling future. Reflect on your values, passions, and strengths to identify areas where you can make a positive impact. Consider volunteering, pursuing a new career path, or engaging in activities that align with your values and allow you to contribute to the well-being of others.

By finding meaning and purpose in your life, you will not only heal from the wounds of narcissistic abuse but also create a sense of fulfillment and satisfaction. Embrace opportunities for personal growth and continue to learn and evolve as an individual. Remember, your past does not define you; it is your resilience and determination to thrive that shape your future.

11.2.6 Inspiring Stories of Survivors: Overcoming and Thriving

Throughout your journey of healing and creating a life of authenticity and fulfillment, it can be incredibly empowering to hear the stories of other survivors who have overcome narcissistic abuse. These stories serve as a reminder that you are not alone and that it is possible to rebuild your life and thrive.

Seek out books, support groups, or online communities where survivors share their experiences and offer support and encouragement. Learn from their triumphs and challenges, and draw inspiration from their resilience. By connecting with others who have walked a similar path, you will find strength and motivation to continue your own journey of healing and growth.

Remember, creating a life of authenticity and fulfillment after narcissistic abuse is a process that takes time and patience. Be gentle with yourself, celebrate your progress, and embrace the opportunities for growth and transformation that lie ahead. You have the power to reclaim your life and create a future filled with joy, purpose, and genuine connections.

11.3 Finding Meaning and Purpose Beyond the Narcissistic Experience

Recovering from a relationship with a narcissist can be an incredibly challenging and painful journey. The emotional and psychological toll it takes on individuals can leave them feeling lost, broken, and questioning their own self-worth. However, it is important to remember that there is life beyond the narcissistic experience, and finding meaning and purpose is not only possible but essential for healing and moving forward.

11.3.1 Rediscovering Your Authentic Self

One of the first steps in finding meaning and purpose beyond the narcissistic experience is reconnecting with your authentic self. Narcissists have a way of manipulating and distorting our sense of identity, causing us to lose sight of who we truly are. Take the time to reflect on your values, passions, and interests that may have been suppressed during the relationship. Engage in activities that bring you joy and allow you to express your true self. This process of rediscovery can be empowering and help you rebuild your self-esteem.

11.3.2 Cultivating Self-Compassion and Forgiveness

Healing from the wounds inflicted by a narcissistic relationship requires practicing self-compassion and forgiveness. Understand that you are not to blame for the narcissist's behavior. It is important to acknowledge and validate your emotions, allowing yourself to grieve and heal. Treat yourself with kindness and compassion, just as you would a dear friend going through a difficult time. Practice forgiveness, not for the narcissist's sake, but for your own peace of mind and emotional well-being.

11.3.3 Embracing Growth and Personal Development

The narcissistic experience can be a catalyst for personal growth and development. Use this opportunity to explore new interests, learn new skills, and challenge yourself to step outside of your comfort zone. Engaging in personal development activities such as therapy, self-help books, or workshops can provide valuable insights and tools for healing and growth. Embrace the journey of self-discovery and allow yourself to evolve into a stronger, more resilient individual.

11.3.4 Building Healthy Relationships

After a narcissistic relationship, it is crucial to establish healthy boundaries and prioritize your emotional well-being. Take the time to reflect on the red flags and warning signs you may have missed in the past. Educate yourself about narcissistic personality styles to avoid falling into similar patterns in future relationships. Surround yourself with supportive and nurturing individuals who respect and value you for who you are. Building healthy relationships based on mutual respect and empathy will contribute to your overall well-being and happiness.

11.3.5 Giving Back and Helping Others

Finding meaning and purpose beyond the narcissistic experience can also involve giving back and helping others who have gone through similar struggles. Sharing your story and supporting others who are on their healing journey can be incredibly empowering and healing for both parties involved. Consider joining support groups, volunteering, or becoming an advocate for raising awareness about narcissistic personality styles. By helping others, you not only contribute to their healing but also reaffirm your own strength and resilience.

11.3.6 Embracing a Life of Authenticity and Fulfillment

Ultimately, finding meaning and purpose beyond the narcissistic experience is about embracing a life of authenticity and fulfillment. It is about reclaiming your power, living according to your values, and pursuing your dreams and aspirations. Surround yourself with positive influences, engage in activities that bring you joy, and prioritize self-care. Remember that you deserve happiness and fulfillment, and by embracing your true self, you can create a life that is meaningful and purposeful.

11.3.7 Inspiring Stories of Survivors: Overcoming and Thriving

Throughout your healing journey, it can be incredibly inspiring and empowering to hear stories of survivors who have overcome the challenges of narcissistic relationships and thrived. Seek out books, podcasts, or support groups where you can connect with others who have walked a similar path. Hearing their stories of resilience and triumph can provide hope and motivation as you navigate your own healing journey.

Remember, healing from a narcissistic relationship takes time and patience. Be gentle with yourself and celebrate every small step forward. By finding meaning and purpose beyond the narcissistic experience, you can reclaim your life, rebuild your self-esteem, and create a future filled with happiness and fulfillment.

11.4 Inspiring Stories of Survivors

In the journey of healing and recovery from narcissistic abuse, it can be incredibly empowering and comforting to hear the stories of others who have walked a similar path. These inspiring stories of survivors serve as a beacon of hope, reminding us that it is possible to overcome the trauma and thrive again. Each survivor's journey is unique, but they all share a common thread of resilience, strength, and the unwavering determination to reclaim their lives. In this section, we will explore some of these inspiring stories, highlighting the lessons learned and the triumphs achieved.

11.4.1 Sarah's Story: Rebuilding Trust in Relationships

Sarah's journey began when she finally recognized the toxic patterns in her relationship with a covert narcissist. She had endured years of emotional manipulation, gaslighting, and a constant erosion of her self-esteem. After finding the courage to leave the relationship, Sarah embarked on a healing journey focused on rebuilding trust in herself and others. Through therapy and self-reflection, she learned to set healthy boundaries, recognize red flags, and trust her instincts. Sarah's story reminds us that even after experiencing the darkest moments, it is possible to find love, trust, and happiness again.

11.4.2 Mark's Story: Creating a Life of Authenticity and Fulfillment

Mark's experience with an overt narcissist left him feeling empty and disconnected from his true self. The constant need for validation and the pressure to conform to the narcissist's expectations had taken a toll on his mental and emotional well-being. However, through therapy and self-discovery, Mark was able to break free from the chains of the narcissistic relationship. He embraced his authentic self, pursued his passions, and surrounded himself with supportive and loving people. Mark's story serves as a reminder that by embracing our true selves, we can create a life filled with purpose, joy, and fulfillment.

11.4.3 Maya's Story: Finding Meaning and Purpose Beyond the Narcissistic Experience

Maya's journey of healing from narcissistic abuse led her to a profound realization – that her experience could be transformed into a catalyst for personal growth and positive change. Through therapy and self-reflection, Maya discovered her inner strength and resilience. She channeled her pain into advocacy work, raising awareness about narcissistic personality styles and supporting other survivors. Maya's story teaches us that even in the face of adversity, we have the power to find meaning and purpose, not only for ourselves but also for the greater good.

11.4.4 Alex's Story: Embracing Growth and Resilience

Alex's experience with a narcissistic boss left him feeling trapped and powerless in the workplace. The constant belittlement and manipulation took a toll on his self-esteem and professional growth. However, Alex refused to let the narcissistic boss define his worth. He sought support from colleagues, developed assertiveness skills, and eventually found the courage to pursue a new career path. Alex's story reminds us that even in challenging environments, we can cultivate resilience, embrace growth, and create a fulfilling professional life.

11.4.5 Emma's Story: Building Healthy Relationships within the GLBTQI Community

Emma's journey as a member of the GLBTQI community navigating narcissistic relationships was filled with unique challenges. She faced societal stereotypes, internalized shame, and the fear of not being accepted for who she truly was. Through therapy and support groups, Emma learned to recognize narcissistic traits in potential partners and build healthy relationships based on mutual respect and understanding. Emma's story highlights the importance of self-acceptance, self-love, and creating a supportive community within the GLBTQI community.

These inspiring stories of survivors demonstrate the resilience and strength of individuals who have faced narcissistic abuse. They serve as a reminder that healing and recovery are possible, and that we are not alone in our experiences. By sharing their stories, these survivors inspire others to break free from the cycle of abuse, reclaim their lives, and thrive once again.

Remember, if you are currently in a narcissistic relationship or have recently left one, it is essential to seek professional help and support. You are not alone, and there is a community of survivors ready to support you on your journey to healing and empowerment.

12

Chapter 12

Conclusion

12.1 Supporting Others

Supporting loved ones who are dealing with narcissistic personality styles can be a challenging and delicate task. It requires empathy, understanding, and a willingness to provide a safe space for them to express their feelings and experiences. In this section, we will explore some strategies and approaches to help you support your loved ones in recognizing and healing from narcissistic relationships.

12.1.1 Creating a Safe and Non-Judgmental Environment

One of the most important aspects of supporting someone who has been in a relationship with a narcissist is creating a safe and non-judgmental environment for them to share their experiences. It is crucial to listen without interrupting or dismissing their feelings. Allow them to express their emotions and validate their experiences. Remember, it is not your role to judge or criticize their choices but to provide support and understanding.

12.1.2 Encouraging Self-Reflection and Awareness

Helping your loved ones recognize the patterns and traits associated with narcissistic personality styles can be a valuable step towards healing. Encourage them to reflect on their past experiences and identify any red flags or warning signs they may have missed. By fostering self-awareness, you can empower them to make healthier choices in their future relationships.

12.1.3 Providing Resources and Education

Supporting your loved ones also involves providing them with resources and education about narcissistic personality styles. Recommend books, articles, or support groups that can help them gain a deeper understanding of the dynamics involved in narcissistic relationships. By arming them with knowledge, you can assist them in making informed decisions and developing strategies for self-protection.

12.1.4 Encouraging Professional Help

In some cases, seeking professional help may be necessary for your loved ones to heal from the effects of narcissistic relationships. Encourage them to consider therapy or counseling with a mental health professional who specializes in trauma and narcissistic abuse. Professional guidance can provide them with the necessary tools and support to navigate their healing journey.

12.1.5 Practicing Self-Care and Boundaries

Supporting others also means taking care of yourself. It is essential to establish and maintain healthy boundaries when supporting someone who has experienced narcissistic abuse. Set limits on the emotional energy you invest and ensure you have time and space for your own well-being. Engage in self-care activities that recharge and rejuvenate you, such as exercise, meditation, or spending time with loved ones.

12.1.6 Encouraging Patience and Understanding

Recovering from narcissistic relationships is a complex and often lengthy process. It is crucial to be patient and understanding with your loved ones as they navigate their healing journey. Recognize that healing is not linear and that they may experience setbacks along the way. Offer your support and understanding, reminding them that their progress is valid and that you are there for them.

12.1.7 Promoting Empowerment and Independence

As your loved ones heal from narcissistic relationships, it is important to encourage their empowerment and independence. Help them rebuild their self-esteem and self-worth by highlighting their strengths and accomplishments. Encourage them to set goals and pursue their passions. By promoting their autonomy, you can assist them in reclaiming their sense of self and moving forward in a positive direction.

12.1.8 Being a Supportive Listener

Above all, being a supportive listener is one of the most valuable ways you can support your loved ones. Allow them to share their experiences, emotions, and thoughts without judgment. Offer a compassionate ear and validate their feelings. Sometimes, all they need is someone who will listen and understand without trying to fix or solve their problems.

Supporting someone who has experienced narcissistic relationships can be emotionally challenging, but it is also incredibly rewarding. By providing a safe and non-judgmental space, encouraging self-reflection, and offering resources and support, you can play a vital role in their healing process. Remember to prioritize your own well-being and practice self-care as you navigate this journey together.

12.2 Advocacy and Education

Advocacy and education play a crucial role in spreading awareness about narcissistic personality styles. By increasing understanding and knowledge about this complex disorder, we can empower individuals to recognize the signs, protect themselves, and support those who have been affected. This chapter will explore the importance of advocacy and education in breaking the cycle of narcissism and promoting healthy relationships.

12.2.1 Spreading Awareness

One of the most effective ways to combat narcissistic personality styles is through advocacy and education. By raising awareness about the traits, behaviors, and impact of narcissism, we can help individuals recognize the signs and seek appropriate support. Advocacy efforts can include public speaking engagements, workshops, and online platforms dedicated to educating the public about narcissistic personality disorder (NPD) and its variations.

12.2.2 Breaking the Stigma

Advocacy and education also aim to break the stigma surrounding narcissistic personality styles. Many individuals who have experienced relationships with narcissists often blame themselves for the abuse they endured. By promoting understanding and empathy, we can help survivors realize that they are not at fault and that narcissistic abuse is a result of the disorder, not their own shortcomings.

12.2.3 Supporting Survivors

Advocacy efforts should focus on providing support and resources for survivors of narcissistic abuse. This can include helplines, support groups, and online communities where individuals can share their experiences and find solace in knowing they are not alone. By creating safe spaces for survivors to heal and connect, we can empower them to rebuild their lives and regain their self-worth.

12.2.4 Educating Professionals

Another crucial aspect of advocacy and education is providing training and resources for professionals who may encounter individuals with narcissistic personality styles. This includes therapists, counselors, and healthcare providers who play a vital role in supporting survivors and helping them navigate the healing process. By equipping professionals with the knowledge and tools to identify and address narcissistic abuse, we can ensure that survivors receive the appropriate care and support they need.

12.2.5 Promoting Healthy Relationships

Advocacy and education also aim to promote healthy relationships and prevent individuals from getting involved with narcissists in the first place. By highlighting the red flags and warning signs of narcissistic personality styles, we can empower individuals to make informed decisions when entering new relationships. This includes recognizing manipulative behaviors, lack of empathy, and a sense of entitlement as potential indicators of narcissism.

12.2.6 Empowering the GLBTQI Community

Advocacy and education should also address the unique challenges faced by the GLBTQI community in relation to narcissistic personality styles. By acknowledging the specific dynamics and experiences within this community, we can provide tailored support and resources. This includes recognizing the impact of societal stereotypes, addressing the intersectionality of identities, and promoting healthy relationship patterns within the GLBTQI community.

12.2.7 Collaborating with Organizations

Advocacy efforts can be strengthened by collaborating with organizations dedicated to raising awareness about narcissistic personality styles. By joining forces with mental health organizations, support groups, and community centers, we can amplify our message and reach a wider audience. This collaboration can include hosting joint events, sharing resources, and providing training opportunities for professionals.

12.2.8 Spreading Awareness Online

In the digital age, online platforms play a significant role in advocacy and education. Social media, blogs, and websites dedicated to narcissistic personality styles can provide valuable information, resources, and support for individuals seeking help. By utilizing these platforms, we can reach a global audience and connect with individuals who may be isolated or unaware of the support available to them.

12.2.9 Advocacy in Schools and Universities

Advocacy and education efforts should extend to schools and universities to ensure that young individuals are equipped with the knowledge and skills to recognize and address narcissistic personality styles. By incorporating this topic into curricula, workshops, and awareness campaigns, we can empower the next generation to build healthy relationships and break the cycle of narcissism.

12.2.10 Inspiring Change

Advocacy and education are powerful tools for inspiring change and creating a society that is more informed and empathetic towards individuals with narcissistic personality styles. By challenging societal norms, promoting empathy, and fostering a culture of healthy relationships, we can create a world where narcissism is recognized, understood, and ultimately diminished.

In conclusion, advocacy and education are essential in spreading awareness about narcissistic personality styles. By breaking the stigma, supporting survivors, and promoting healthy relationships, we can empower individuals to recognize the signs, protect themselves, and create a society that is more informed and compassionate. Through collaborative efforts and the utilization of various platforms, we can inspire change and break the cycle of narcissism.

12.3 Promoting Healthy Relationships

Promoting healthy relationships is essential in breaking the cycle of narcissism and fostering emotional well-being. By understanding the traits and dynamics of narcissistic personality styles, individuals can equip themselves with the knowledge and tools necessary to identify and avoid toxic relationships. In this chapter, we will explore strategies for promoting healthy relationships, both in romantic and non-romantic contexts, and discuss ways to create a supportive and nurturing environment.

12.3.1 Identifying and Avoiding Narcissistic Relationships

Recognizing the red flags and early warning signs of narcissistic personality styles is crucial in avoiding toxic relationships. While it is important to approach new relationships with an open mind, it is equally important to be aware of certain behaviors that may indicate narcissistic tendencies. Some common red flags include:

1. Excessive self-centeredness: Narcissists often prioritize their own needs and desires above others, displaying a lack of empathy and consideration for others.

2. Grandiose sense of self-importance: They may have an inflated sense of their own abilities and achievements, constantly seeking admiration and validation from others.

3. Manipulative behavior: Narcissists may use manipulation tactics such as gaslighting, guilt-tripping, and emotional blackmail to control and dominate their partners.

4. Lack of accountability: They may refuse to take responsibility for their actions, often blaming others for their mistakes or shortcomings.

5. Intense need for attention and admiration: Narcissists crave constant attention and validation, often seeking it from multiple sources.

6. Lack of boundaries: They may disregard personal boundaries and invade the privacy of others, displaying a sense of entitlement.

To avoid getting involved in a narcissistic relationship, it is important to trust your instincts and set healthy boundaries. Take the time to get to know someone before committing to a relationship, and observe how they treat others. Engage in open and honest communication, and be wary of any signs of manipulation or disregard for your feelings and needs. Remember, it is better to be single and happy than to be in a toxic relationship.

12.3.2 Nurturing Healthy Relationships

Building and maintaining healthy relationships requires effort and commitment from both parties involved. Here are some strategies for promoting healthy relationships:

1. Effective Communication: Open and honest communication is the foundation of any healthy relationship. Express your needs, concerns, and boundaries clearly, and encourage your partner to do the same. Active listening and empathy are essential in fostering understanding and resolving conflicts.

2. Mutual Respect: Respect is the cornerstone of a healthy relationship. Treat your partner with kindness, consideration, and respect their boundaries. Value their opinions and perspectives, and avoid belittling or demeaning behavior.

3. Emotional Support: Provide emotional support to your partner and be

there for them during both the good and challenging times. Validate their feelings and experiences, and offer a safe space for them to express themselves without judgment.

4. Healthy Boundaries: Establish and maintain healthy boundaries in your relationship. Respect each other's personal space, interests, and individuality. Encourage independence and allow each other to pursue personal goals and interests.

5. Shared Values and Goals: Find common ground and shared values with your partner. Aligning your goals and aspirations can create a strong foundation for a healthy and fulfilling relationship.

6. Self-Care: Prioritize self-care and ensure that you are taking care of your own emotional and physical well-being. Nurture your own interests, hobbies, and friendships outside of the relationship. Remember, a healthy relationship should enhance your life, not consume it.

12.3.3 Breaking the Cycle of Narcissism

Breaking the cycle of narcissism involves not only promoting healthy relationships but also raising awareness and educating others about narcissistic personality styles. By sharing our knowledge and experiences, we can help others recognize and understand the dynamics of narcissistic relationships. Here are some ways to promote healthy relationships and break the cycle of narcissism:

1. Education and Awareness: Spread awareness about narcissistic personality styles through conversations, social media, and community events. Educate others about the red flags and warning signs of narcissistic behavior, and provide resources for support and healing.

2. Support and Empathy: Offer support and empathy to individuals who have experienced narcissistic abuse. Create a safe and non-judgmental space for them to share their stories and seek guidance. Encourage them to seek professional help if needed.

3. Role Modeling Healthy Relationships: Lead by example and demon-

strate what a healthy relationship looks like. Show empathy, respect, and kindness in your interactions with others. By modeling healthy behaviors, you can inspire others to do the same.

4. Encouraging Self-Reflection: Encourage individuals to engage in self-reflection and introspection. Help them explore their own patterns and behaviors in relationships, and support them in making positive changes.

5. Building Support Networks: Foster a sense of community and support by connecting individuals who have experienced narcissistic abuse. Encourage them to share their stories, provide validation, and offer guidance to one another.

By promoting healthy relationships and raising awareness about narcissistic personality styles, we can create a society that values empathy, respect, and emotional well-being. Together, we can break the cycle of narcissism and foster healthier and more fulfilling connections with others.

12.4 The Journey Continues

As you reach the end of this book, it is important to acknowledge that the journey of understanding and surviving narcissistic personality styles is an ongoing one. Healing and recovery take time, and it is crucial to embrace growth and resilience as you continue on your path towards a healthier and happier life.

12.4.1 Embracing Personal Growth

The experience of being in a relationship with a narcissist can be incredibly challenging and traumatic. It is important to remember that healing is a process, and it is normal to have ups and downs along the way. Embracing personal growth means acknowledging your own strength and resilience, and allowing yourself to learn and grow from the experience.

One key aspect of personal growth is self-reflection. Take the time to reflect on the patterns and dynamics that led you into a relationship with a narcissist. This self-awareness will help you identify any vulnerabilities or patterns that may have made you susceptible to their manipulation. By understanding these patterns, you can work towards breaking free from them and developing healthier relationship patterns in the future.

Another important aspect of personal growth is self-compassion and forgiveness. It is common for survivors of narcissistic abuse to blame themselves for the relationship's failure or for falling victim to the narcissist's manipulation. However, it is crucial to remember that narcissists are skilled manipulators who prey on vulnerabilities. Be kind to yourself and recognize that you are not to blame for the narcissist's actions.

12.4.2 Building Resilience

Building resilience is an essential part of the healing process. It involves developing the ability to bounce back from adversity and to cope with future challenges. Here are some strategies to help you build resilience:

1. **Develop a support network**: Surround yourself with people who understand and support you. Seek out friends, family, or support groups who can provide a safe space for you to share your experiences and emotions.

2. **Practice self-care**: Prioritize your physical, emotional, and mental well-being. Engage in activities that bring you joy and relaxation. Take care of your body through exercise, healthy eating, and adequate rest. Make time for self-reflection and self-care practices such as meditation or journaling.

3. **Set healthy boundaries**: Establish clear boundaries with others and learn to say no when necessary. This will help protect your emotional well-being and prevent you from being taken advantage of in future relationships.

4. **Seek professional help**: Consider seeking therapy or counseling to help you navigate the healing process. A trained professional can

provide guidance, support, and tools to help you overcome the effects of narcissistic abuse.

5. **Practice self-empowerment**: Take control of your own life and make choices that align with your values and goals. Focus on your strengths and celebrate your achievements, no matter how small they may seem.

12.4.3 Spreading Awareness and Empowering Others

As you continue on your journey of healing and growth, you may find it empowering to share your story and raise awareness about narcissistic personality styles. By doing so, you can help others recognize the signs of narcissistic abuse and provide support to those who may be going through similar experiences. Here are some ways you can make a difference:

1. **Supporting loved ones**: Share your knowledge and experiences with friends and family members who may be in relationships with narcissists. Offer a listening ear and provide resources that can help them understand and navigate their own situations.

2. **Advocacy and education**: Consider becoming an advocate for survivors of narcissistic abuse. Raise awareness by sharing your story through social media, blogs, or public speaking engagements. Educate others about the signs of narcissistic personality styles and the impact they can have on individuals and relationships.

3. **Promoting healthy relationships**: Break the cycle of narcissism by promoting healthy relationship dynamics. Encourage open communication, empathy, and mutual respect in all types of relationships. Support organizations and initiatives that focus on promoting healthy relationships and preventing narcissistic abuse.

4. **Inspiring others**: Share stories of survivors who have overcome narcissistic abuse and thrived. By highlighting these inspiring stories, you can provide hope and encouragement to those who may be struggling on their own healing journey.

Remember, the journey of understanding and surviving narcissistic personality styles is unique to each individual. It is important to be patient with yourself and to seek support when needed. By embracing personal growth, building resilience, and empowering others, you can create a positive impact not only in your own life but also in the lives of those around you.